$4.95

W9-BFJ-402

ENERGY SAVING DECORATING

By Judy Lindahl

Illustrated by Laurie Adam

To Whitney, age 3, and Heather, age 1, (without whom this book might have been completed much sooner)—I LOVE YOU!

Special thanks to Bev Groshens, Pauline Gorger, Karen Dillon, Jim Chumbley, Chuck Pringle, Eleanor Malin.

Brand names are mentioned in this book only to indicate consumer products which I have personally used and with which I have been pleased. I am not subsidized by anyone and there may very well be other products that are comparable or even better about which I am unaware.

Copyright © 1981, Judy Lindahl
Published by Judy Lindahl, 3211 NE Siskiyou, Portland, OR 97212

Second Printing

All rights reserved. No part of this book may be reproduced in any form without permisison in writing from the author, except by a reviewer who may quote brief passages in review.

ISBN 0-9603032-3-5
Library of Congress No. 81-90134

Printed in USA

About the Author: Judy Lindahl is a home economist residing in Portland, Oregon. She was graduated from Washington State University with honors and received her B.S. in Home Economics Education. She taught home economics in Beaverton, Oregon for several years before leaving to join the educational staff at Simplicity Pattern Co., Inc. of New York. As an educational fashion stylist Judy traveled the country presenting programs in schools and for 4-H, extension, and consumer groups for five and a half years. In 1973 she created a program of ideas and inspiration for do-it-yourself decorators which she has presented across the country and in Canada. She is the author and publisher of Decorating with Fabric/An Idea Book and The Shade Book (Paperbacks) which grew out of the programs, and Decorating with Fabric, (a hardback for Butterick Publishing). Judy has been involved in writing, demonstration and television work for Fieldcrest sheets. Currently Judy lectures and travels on a free lance basis. She is married and the mother of two daughters and has been featured in Outstanding Young Women of America and Personalities of the West and Midwest.

TABLE OF CONTENTS

INTRODUCTION

For years I have been an absolute believer in the joys and benefits of do-it-yourself decorating, especially where fabric is concerned. I have spent a good many years teaching others, hoping to impart some of the excitement and enthusiasm I find for myself; trying to erase the fear of failure and instill the thrill of success.

In the past few years part of me had begun to question the energy efficiency of many decorating tricks and techniques. Then, more recently and following the heels of some unusually cold Oregon weather, a friend asked if I would give a short speech on energy wise decorating for a state home economists meeting. "Sure, I can do that," I replied, thinking I could easily fill my time with some information about roller and Roman shades (another subject dear to my heart.)

But as I began to research the subject and think seriously about this whole energy issue, I realized that MOST OF US DON'T. We really only get serious about energy when it is our own pocketbook that is severely pinched. Another problem is that energy-savings has become a catch word used to advertise almost anything. How can we make good, sound, valid, decisions when we are being bombarded with products and information? It requires patience, thoughtfulness, and a willingness to learn and synthesize information and ideas.

Although testing and research go on daily in the area of energy savings—it still is not an exact science in many cases. Because each house, each location, each situation is so different, it is nearly impossible to quote numbers and statistics that would be valid for everyone. One must learn to evaluate and make judgments for his own individual situation.

To be honest, energy saving decorating should not have top priority in your energy plan. First comes improving insulation in ceilings and floors, and caulking and weatherstripping to stop air leaks and infiltration. Some of this may be accomplished along with decorating—but it should take first priority. Then, no doubt, you will turn to windows and other areas for conservation. The point is, most of us will be decorating or re-decorating most of our lives. So why not be energy conscious and create an AESTHETIC AND EFFICIENT PLAN. If we do—we will all benefit.

As in my previous books I have attempted to put together a collection of thoughts and ideas which you may use, combine, or which hopefully may inspire you to create your own solutions. This should be a resource to use over and over to help with different situations. We all need our minds jogged now and then to get us thinking and moving. From time to time material in this book will be updated, revised, or deleted as new products and research make necessary. I am also interested in hearing from readers about ideas they have tried and found successful.

This book does not list every energy product available, nor have I dealt with items requiring construction or remodeling. That is a task others are doing well. (See Suggested Reading.) Further, with new products and ideas appearing almost daily—it would be a formidable task at best. Rather you will find suggestions of ways to combine small details in your decorating plans, which when added together can equal larger energy savings.

Remember—there is simply no aspect of decorating right now that is quite so critical and beneficial to us all as ENERGY SAVING DECORATING.

GETTING STARTED
—A New Attitude

Without doubt almost all of us will decorate a room, an apartment, a home—or several of each during our lifetime. In the past the main consideration was usually aesthetic; what we LIKED best and what LOOKED good to us.

Statistics show we moved often, which meant decorating often, too. But soaring costs and the energy squeeze are causing many of us to stay home more, stay in one place longer, and decorate less often. Thus today's decorating, of necessity, must meet many criteria: How long can I live with this? How long will these furnishings last? What can I do seasonally, or occasionally to give a new look or feeling? Is what I am doing energy efficient? How can I make what I already own more efficient?

To some degree our thinking and taste will have to be re-shaped. We will need to realize that there may be several approaches to a problem—some more energy efficient than others. To be most effective we need to learn to analyze each step from the energy point of view. Think it over from every direction—is there something you can do to create more efficiency? What? Are there several choices? The one you choose will probably be a compromise of what is acceptable aesthetically and energy efficient, too. I don't believe that aesthetics must always be sacrificed for efficiency. In some cases, perhaps. But in general by careful thought and wise planning —I think it is possible to save energy and like the look of things, too. We will, however, need to learn to accept things that look 'different' than styles we have grown up with.

Whether you are decorating 'from scratch' or up-dating an existing environment, the point is, there are things you CAN do. Energy savings is not something to fear, or ignore. Consider it a challenge—make it your goal to do what you can . . . step-by-step, bit-by-bit, room-by-room. Always be looking for ideas that can be adapted into your decorating lifestyle.

HINT: Keep a file folder, box, scrapbook, or drawer where you can clip and save information and articles on energy savings that you find appealing and intriguing. You may not need them now and they may not apply to your situation now, but they won't be lost or misplaced when you do need them.

I am currently working on re-decorating a good portion of our "new" older home. As I have begun to develop the scheme and plans—I am evaluating each point as I go. I know if I selected EVERY SINGLE color, treatment, accessory, etc. for its efficiency only—that we might not be happy with the end result. But everywhere I can—I'm striving to incorporate ideas and treatments, particularly at windows, that are efficient as well as appealing.

A practical way to get started is to work on one room at a time. Analyze each point, evaluate what and how much you can do. Keep a notebook for jotting down your decorating ideas. Be sure to jot down your energy ideas, too, before they slip away and are forgotten.

LET'S GET IT DONE . . .

When it comes to energy efficient decorating then, the point is I can do it! You can do it! We can all do it! We just have to get busy and try!

PSYCHO- LOGICAL DECORATING

PSYCHOLOGICAL WHAT?

Stop! Don't let the title frighten you away. Here is one aspect of our decorating we often completely overlook—and it can be a very important one. Psychological decorating can play a surprisingly large role in how comfortable or uncomfortable we feel at any given temperature setting. If we can set our thermostats at 65° and enjoy the benefits of fuel savings, and still FEEL several degrees warmer or cooler, then it's worth examining.

Even though you have your general plan of decorating already selected, why not relate it to the following points and see if there are some areas where you can let a little psychology warm you up—or cool you down.

How can color, lines, textures, spaces, lighting, etc., affect your comfort? It is often difficult to extract one point from the other, since a room logically is a blend of many. But by analyzing each point separately you may better be able to see how they affect each other, and how the sum of the parts equals the total effect. Then by adding or subtracting certain effects you may better create the feeling or mood you are working toward.

WARM VS COOL COLORS

PSYCHOLOGICAL EFFECTS OF COLOR

Using the psychology of color to create a feeling of warmth or coolness has long been a favorite technique in decorating. It takes on added significance as we contemplate the effects of energy saved.

Color has strong emotional and personal effects on people. Many studies have been conducted and reported about reactions to color in situations where color is the only factor of change. For example:

- Cafeterias or factory work areas painted green have drawn complaints of "turn up the thermostat" from workers. But when the same rooms are painted a warm yellow or orange complaints cease. Only the color has changed, not the thermostat.
- Pulse rate and blood pressure can be reduced in the presence of cool colors.
- Some athletic directors paint home team dressing rooms bright red and orange, visitors' rooms pale blue.

- Time seems to pass faster for patients in warm colored rooms than when rooms are painted in cool colors.
- A black bridge frequently was the choice for suicide attempts. The rate dropped when the bridge was painted green.
- Factory workers complained about the weight of heavy tool boxes which were brown. Repainting them a light color stopped the complaints.

To better understand color and how its psychological effects can be the best utilized, it helps to have a basic color background.

THREE DIMENSIONS OF COLOR

All colors have three dimensions that play a part in how they are perceived: Hue, Value, and Intensity.

HUE: The name of a color. Green, blue, yellow, red are hues.

VALUE: The darkness (shade) of a color achieved by adding varying amounts of black, or the lightness (tint) of a color achieved by adding varying amounts of white. Forest green is a dark value (shade) of green; mint or seafoam are light values (tints).

INTENSITY: The brightness or dullness of a color relative to the amount of pure color it contains. Khaki green is a dull yellow-green while chartreuse is an intense yellow-green. To dull a color, its complement, that is, its opposite on a color wheel is added in varying amounts.

NOTE: To help you get a feeling for which of several colors might be of lighter or darker value, without the distraction of hue or intensity, squint your eyes to eliminate as much light and hue as possible. Thus you will be looking at the colors in terms of grayness—light or dark. I play this game a lot when selecting prints or by putting several fabric pieces side by side to see if values are creating contrast or blending.

THE COLOR WHEEL

Hues (colors) can be organized by a number of different systems into warm and cool categories. One of the most common is the color wheel devised by Sir David Brewster.

Placing basic colors in a wheel configuration makes it easy to see the relationship of warm and cool.

Colors in the warm side of the wheel are the colors of sun, heat, fire—hence their warm psychological effect on us. The cool colors of blue, green, violet are colors of water, sky, shadow, ice. Two colors, yellow-green and red-violet may be considered to be transitional. That is, they may take on warmer or cooler feelings depending whether they are mixed with a scheme of blue/green or violet/red/orange. Thus in rooms that are given a seasonal decorating change (see p. 28), these colors might be useful to help make the change from warm to cool in a seasonal decorating plan.

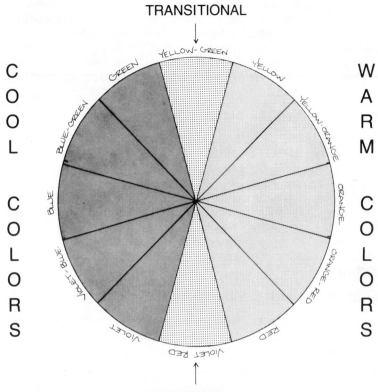

TRANSITIONAL

COOL COLORS

WARM COLORS

TRANSITIONAL

Once the basics of colors are understood, it is easier to see how to create desired effects by manipulating the hue, value, and intensity. Try taking colors you plan to use, plug them into the chart and see what the effect will be.

EFFECTS OF HUE-VALUE-INTENSITY

	WARM	COOL
HUE	Red, Yellow, Orange Stimulating, energetic	Blue, Green, Violet Restful, quiet
VALUE	High (light) = tints spring green	Low (dark) = shades forest green
INTENSITY	Bright (strong) royal blue	Dull (weak) navy

In general warm colors are best selected for north facing rooms and cool colors for south and west. East is generally considered more neutral, leaving the choices open to other influencing factors, including the amount and type of light the rooms receive.

13

But what if these guidelines are contrary to your own color furnishings or preferences? Then think through some alternatives—ways to use color, or other psychological and physical factors that can offset your color choices. For example you love blue for a bedroom color, but your room faces north. Paint it blue, but warm it up with lavish use of yellow or another warm color. Or use a 'warmer' blue—one with a yellow base tone and not an icy looking tint. Select a medium to darker value and slightly higher intensity.

The Color Key System®

In 1950 Robert Dorr created a color system for use in coordinating colors to achieve better harmony. His method, called the Color Key System®, is now owned by the Ameritone Color Key Corporation. All colors are divided into two groups called Key One or Key Two. Colors in Key One have a blue base and colors in Key Two have a yellow base. Thus beiges like oyster, cream, champagne, mirage, (or any other color) will have cool or warm undertones depending which key they are in. Color coordination becomes simple since colors in one key will always harmonize with other colors in the same key. But a discordant feeling can be created when a scheme mixes colors from the two Keys.

NOTE: This theory can be used in makeup and wardrobe planning as well.

A home decorated in one key will have a more flowing harmony than one that shifts keys from room to room. However, this is not as important as keeping the same key within a room.

One way to check the Color Key of any item is to use a purse or pocket directory of colors developed for this purpose. It fans out to show 424 colors. You may purchase your own directory by writing for information to: Video Systems Network, Inc., PO Box 3278, Culver City, CA 90230.

Sources for Color Schemes

The source or the idea for your color scheme can come from any number of places. It helps to keep clippings and photos in an idea notebook of things that particularly appeal to you.

NOTE: If your room has dark wood paneling, use paint or fabric colors that are rather intense because the dark wood will absorb color.

WARM VS. COOL LIGHTING

Just as a feeling of warmth or coolness can be achieved through use of color, you can create a similar mood and feeling with lighting. Natural and artificial lighting have color characteristics that can be used to advantage.

Consider how the sun strikes the rooms in your home as the day progresses. The sun at noon for example is closest to white light, which yields the truest color quality. North light, used often by artists, is cool and steady with few shifting shadows. East light, first morning light, shifts from bright to neutral as the day advances. South light seems warm and constantly shifts during the day. West light can be very warm and rich, particularly in late afternoon. The level of light affects us psychologically with bright lighting creating feelings of cheer, warmth, and high physical and mental energy. We feel cooler, more tranquil and rested in dim lighting. Thus the thoughtful placement of light fixtures and dimmer controls can contribute to our ability to adjust levels of lighting and mood.

Artificial lighting consists mainly of a choice or blend of incandescent and fluorescent. The energy factor of lighting is discussed later. Here we are concerned with the psychological effects of heat and color.

Incandescent

Incandescent lamps cast a warm yellowish-white glow and radiate heat as they burn (90% of energy used in lamps is heat, 10% is light). They strengthen warm colors (red, orange, yellow), grey or dull blue tones, and give complexions a warm ruddy glow. Incandescent lamps are available in colors (pink, blue, green, yellow) for special effects though they have a much lower lumen output and may be unacceptable for general lighting. If special colors are not generally available they may be found in specialty lighting stores.

Fluorescent

Fluorescent lighting radiates less heat into a room than incandescent and is available in half a dozen colors. The most common colors used in home interiors include Deluxe Warm White (soft white) and Deluxe Cool White. The term deluxe refers to color and not to cost. Deluxe Warm White is usually recommended for homes where illumination will be fairly low and the atmosphere will be primarily 'social.' It is closest to incandescent light in its rendering. It gives a warming effect on the atmosphere and strengthens red, orange, yellow, and green colors. It dulls or greys blue tones and gives a ruddy glow to complexions.

Cool White Deluxe most simulates natural daylight and neutral or cooler atmosphere with a white light that tends to render most all colors well. There are even newer more 'fine-tuned' high color lamps—i.e. 'Chromaline'™ by G.E., 'Incandescent/Fluorescent' by Sylvania, and 'Living White' by Westinghouse.

In general, to achieve color harmony in a room, either 'match' warm light on warm colors, or cool light on cool colors, to create a bright, clear effect; or 'mix' warm light on cool colors or cool light on warm colors for a subdued greyed effect.

NOTE: Because natural daylight, incandescent, or fluorescent light can each have a different effect on the way a color is perceived by the human eye, it is always important to test colors and fabrics you are considering for your decorating scheme. Try to observe them in your own home at different times of the day and under the different types of lighting you usually use or are considering. It is also possible to alter the appearance and effect of some lights by the use of filters or shades. For example, a lampshade in a fabric with warm yellow tones will add its own warm glow to the alredy warm glow of incandescent lighting.

The following excerpt from Light and Color by General Electric helps to explain why some types and colors of lights have limited availability and why home lighting in general leans toward warm tones.

> "Selecting a 'white' light source on the basis of its color appearance or its color rendering properties alone is rarely done for general lighting. . . . Incandescent lamps generally are considered to have a slight edge over other lamps in color rendering—not because they render colors more naturally, but because through decades of usage, they have come to be CONSIDERED the norm. 'GOOD' rendition is generally interpreted to mean the 'FAMILIAR' appearance of familiar objects— and objects assume 'familiar' colors only by being frequently seen under certain types of light sources (daylight or incandescent). If fluorescent lamps had come into wide usage before incandescents, it is possible that object colors would appear most 'familiar' under them—instead of incandescents."

Unfortunately, lighting is often added to our decor as an afterthought. Yet its importance in color, mood and emotion is obvious. We need to be more willing to experiment and be open to new effects and techniques.

| Lamp Names | FLUORESCENT LAMPS | | | | INCANDESCENT |
	Cool* White	Deluxe* Cool White	Warm** White	Deluxe** Warm White	Filament**
Efficacy (Lumens/watt)	High	Medium	High	Medium	Low
Lamp appearance effect on neutral surfaces	White	White	Yellowish white	Yellowish white	Yellowish white
Effect on "atmosphere"	Neutral to moderately cool	Neutral to moderately cool	Warm	Warm	Warm
Colors strengthened	Orange, Yellow, Blue	All nearly equal	Orange, Yellow	Red, Orange Yellow, Green	Red Orange Yellow
Colors greyed	Red	None appreciably	Red, Green	Blue	Blue
Effect on complexions	Pale Pink	Most natural	Sallow	Ruddy	Ruddiest
Remarks	Blends with natural daylight—Good color acceptance	Best overall color rendition; simulates natural daylight	Blends with incandescent light—poor color acceptance	Good color rendition; simulates incandescent light	Good color rendering

*Greater preference at higher levels   **Greater preference at lower levels.

Photo James Seeman Studios, Wallcovering: A Div. of MASONITE Corp.

SOFT, WARM TEXTURES and the look of quilted walls create a warm environment. Cool it down with slipcovers and accessories.

Photo Courtesy of Naugahyde®/Uniroyal Coated Fabrics

A STORAGE MODULE ON CASTERS acts as a wall to divide space and create a warm, cozy area. Roll it to a new location to open up a cool, spacious feeling.

COZY VS. SPARE DECORATING

Studies show that rooms decorated to give a feeling of coziness also tend to impart a feeling of warmth. The American Society of Heating, Refrigerating and Air Conditioning Engineers tested people in a cozy and a sparsely decorated room. Though tests showed that skin temperature was the same in each—people reported feeling warmer by several degrees (as much as 2.5 degrees in one study) in the cozier atmosphere. By contrast, a very spread out room arrangement fosters feelings of spaciousness and draftiness which can make one feel cooler.

COZY (Warm)　　　　**VS**　　　　**SPARE (Cool)**

1. Plump rounded lines	1. Clean straight lines
2. Lots of accessories and collectibles	2. Few Accessories
3. More individual pieces	3. Fewer furnishings or single-look modules
4. Broken spaces	4. Open spaces
5. Low ceilings	5. High ceilings
6. Covered windows	6. Uncovered windows

COVERED WALLS VS. PAINTED WALLS

Walls may be covered in a variety of ways—fabric, wallcoverings: (paper, mylar, grasscloth, cork). This addition of texture adds an air of warmth and coziness, which can be heightened or decreased depending upon the amount of color, design, or texture. When furniture and accessories are covered in the same or coordinated fabric, the effect is increased. Pillows, folding or decorative screens, window shades, lamp shades, planters, window treatments, picture frames are logical extensions of this decorating theme.

Photo Courtesy of Collins & Aikman. United Wallcoverings; Collins & Aikman carpet.

Wood paneling generally contributes to a feeling of warmth or coziness. Part of the reason stems from the fact that a majority of wood paneling is in the warmer color range.

NOTE: See DECORATING WITH FABRIC/An Idea Book for more ideas and information on how to apply fabric to walls. Also see how-to suggestions in later chapter of this book.

In general painted walls give a cooler background to a room than wall-coverings. This feeling is increased if walls are lacquered or enameled or given a marbleized treatment. Tile, marble, or smooth plastic laminates also create coolness. It is the combination of the feeling of smooth, shiny, and hard that psychologically makes us visualize a cool image.

Photo Courtesy of Armstrong Cork Company

PADDED VS. STRUCTURAL

Extra padding can make a difference in how we perceive our surroundings. In general we feel warmer when we surround ourselves with softer, fuller, textured fabrics, furniture and carpets. A decidedly cooler atmosphere is achieved with sleek, smooth, spare surfaces.

WALLS: The high tech look of 'mover's pads' applied to walls not only insulates and adds texture and warmth, it can hide a multitude of sins as far as the condition of the walls beneath. Cracks, rough surface, stains, pipes, even doors and windows can be concealed with careful application.

Walls can be 'upholstered' by adding a layer of polyester fleece (Pellon)® Thermolam 'Plus' (Stacy) needlepunch, quilt batting or foam. Ready quilted fabrics (some have foam filling), bedspreads, comforters, drapery fabrics are another excellent source of the padded look for walls.

FURNISHINGS: The rounder, softer, fuller upholstered looks are gaining in popularity and contribute to a warm, comfortable feeling. For coolness, contrast their effect with spare, square, clean lines. Comforters and quilts add texture when used as tablecloths and runners, slipcovers, pillows, even window hangings.

FLOORS: The texture, softness, and insulating value of carpeting vs. uncovered wood, vinyl, tile, slate or marble flooring will come under more scrutiny by the energy conscious. Brick and quarry tile do give some feeling of warmth due to their warm rust colors and when properly planned and installed can be used to retain heat in passive solar applications.

It is not unusual to see carpeting used on walls and platforms to take advantage of insulating and sound dampening qualities.

NOTE: If you live in a climate of extremes, you might choose hard floors with loose-lay carpet or area rugs that could be taken up during summer months.

COVERED VS. UNCOVERED WINDOWS

Psychologically people feel warmer when drapes, shades or some type of covering is placed over bare glass at night. Though actual temperatures remain constant, the smooth, black expanse of window creates a colder feeling than a covered window. In addition, drapes or shades are closer to room temperature, thus reducing the loss of body heat radiation to the cooler surface. Moreover, most home heating systems do not measure the temperature at the window itself. The temperature at the window surface of a room where the thermostat is set at 75° F. may actually be ten to fifteen degrees cooler.

Photo Courtesy of Ethan Allen

If the uncovered window is a favorite in your decorating plan, you will need to consider double glazing at the minimum (two panes of glass installed back to back with an air space between them). Probably some type of outside shading will be incorporated for warm climates. It would also be wise to consider some type of movable insulation which could either be stored when not in seasonal use or inconspicuously installed so it is available as needed for hottest and coldest days.

Photo Courtesy of Van Luit & Co., Photography: George R. Szanik

PRINT VS. PLAIN

As a general rule prints and free flowing designs contribute more to the feeling of warmth or coziness. Geometrics, plain colors and smooth textures impart the feeling of space, openness, smoothness, and hard finish that psychologically translate to cool feelings.

Photo Courtesy of James Seeman Studios. Wallcovering; A Div. of MASONITE Corp.

It is a good idea to keep in mind the importance of color when selecting prints and designs. If there is a choice between a color blend you love and a design (in wrong colors) you love, go for the color. You can adjust to a design, but you cannot adjust as easily to color because it affects you all the time, subjectively.

Print mixing generally creates more warmth or coziness, although this is also very dependent upon colors used in the prints. There are many fabric and wallcovering collections being designed today with from three to twelve prints that can be mixed together for a cohesive look.

Photo Courtesy of Armstrong Cork Company

A COZY, WARM FEELING is created through visual and textural techniques. Napped, soft fabrics feel warm to the touch. Warm colors for area carpet and pillow accents add to the mood.

The Case For . . . SEASONAL DECORATING

You can raise or lower the apparent temperature of a room by utilizing a seasonal decorating plan just as great-grandmother used to practice when rugs were rolled up and stored in the summer, the heavy drapes came down and gave way to simpler, airier window treatments, and crisp slipcovers gave furnishings a cooler look and feel. Seasonal decorating was standard procedure, the changes gave an emotional lift, refreshed the eye, and made furnishings last longer, too. Then along came air conditioning and cheap heat and seasonal decorating got lost in the shuffle. Its rebirth may take a bit of attitude adjustment for some, but it makes a lot of sense and cents, too.

Cooling a Room

TO CREATE A COOL FEELING quilted chair throws are removed. A smooth, cool, shiny fabric slipcover is tucked and tied over the sofa. Uncovered table and windows, more plants, cool fans and accessories contribute, too.

When people think of seasonal decorating, they usually think of summerizing. But with the popularity of rattan, wicker, small scale furnishings, many 'temporary' pieces becoming somewhat permanent, AND the soaring costs of heat, the trend may be to consider what can be done to winterize decor. Adding padding or coziness with quilted or textured throws, easy slipcovers, table covers, runners, comforters, screens, pillows, padded art, area rugs, etc. can be easily accomplished. The texture of fabrics can provide insulation in the winter through the thermal resistance of the fabric and the air film around it. (This principle is important in the layering of clothes in the winter, too.) Carpets, wall hangings and insulated draperies all increase the actual R-value (resistance to heat and cold) of the exterior surfaces.

HOW TO ACHIEVE SEASONAL DECORATING

WARMING IT UP		COOLING IT DOWN
• Use area rugs on carpets or wood floors. Warm colors and/or textures.	FLOORS	• Remove rugs for bare floors or cool-look carpet. Bleached wood or light color tile or flooring beneath.
• Drapes or layered curtain and shade window treatments, shutters with shades, cornices, valances.	WINDOWS	• Light drapes or remove drapes and use shades, shutters, sheer curtains, or folding screens.
• Warm colors and/or textured upholstery. Fabric that feels warm. Quilted fabrics, brushed and napped surfaces.	UPHOLSTERY	• Crisp, cool, smooth, fabrics and colors for slipcovers. Cotton, canvas, glazed chintz, linen are good choices.
• Fewer plants, ceramic pots • Quilts, hooked rugs, soft sculptured, darker and warmer colored art. • Warm, textured pillows.	ACCESSORIES	• Massed plants, use basket or reed pot covers. • Light, airy, open, prints, posters or fabric hangings. • Cool color pillow covers.
• Incandescent light gives warmer colors and more heat; highlights warm colors, dulls cool colors. Fluorescent (Warm White Deluxe) uses less energy, gives more light.	LIGHTING	• Try cool color lighting (fluorescent) in living spaces, but not kitchens, because of color effects on red tones. Cool White Deluxe accents cool colors and dulls warm colors.

Furniture should be arranged to avoid drafts near doors and windows and other cool spots in the home. In warmer climates furnishings should be placed to catch air currents. In winter objects should be placed in the sun's path to absorb heat and radiate it back later. Conversely, in warm weather windows should be shaded and furniture arranged to prevent heat damage or absorption. Furniture should not block air circulation around radiators, heating ducts, air conditioners, or baseboard heaters.

NOTE: Since we are encouraged to uncover windows in winter to take advantage of solar heat gain, some windows may need treatments with shades of materials that stop ultra-violet rays (which fade furnishings) while letting heat in.

Winter Mode

Conceal Fireplace in Summer

Though the problem of storage for seasonal items is certainly something to be considered—it is not an insurmountable obstacle. If attic or closet space is unavailable, space can sometimes be found under beds, beneath long tablecloths, in benches or trunks, behind folding screens, overhead in garages, or in 'created' instant closets that steal a few inches in a corner somewhere.

Instant Closet: Build a framework of 1″ × 2″ (2,5x5 cm) lumber, wrap and staple fabric around frames (see shutter construction p. 76). Finish back if desired, with muslin. Hinge to wall. Add magnetic catch. Or use solid wood boards and piano hinges, or add magnetic catches to ceiling and floor frame and set panels in place against the catches.

WINDOWS

In the average home 15 to 30 percent of the heat is lost through the windows. If your home has many large windows that figure could be 45 per cent or more. But studies by the Dept. of Energy solar lab at Los Alamos, N.M. show that with proper window insulation the average structure can reduce its winter heating bill by up to 40 per cent, and cut air conditioning costs in half. So, once you have insulated ceilings and weather-stripped and caulked to stop air leaks, you will undoubtedly turn some of your attention and decorating dollars to the windows.

The window treatments you choose can help to insulate windows. They therefore become movable insulation, since they can be opened or removed during the day to let light and solar heat enter.

Picture yourself holding a drinking glass in one hand and a styrofoam cup in the other. Have both filled with boiling coffee. You can imagine how many seconds you could hold the glass as the heat pours through to burn your hand, but the foam cup retains nearly all the heat so you can comfortably hold it. The same relationship of heat/cold and your comfort is true of windows. In essence, window insulation is like the styrofoam cup.

NOTE: It should be stated right up front that to be effective, any system or addition must be carefully installed, well sealed, and it MUST BE USED.

Making some comparisons of R-values (resistance to heat flow including winter heat loss and summer heat gain) can help to emphasize the need for window insulation:

A well insulated ceiling may have	R 38
A stud wall with 3½″ *(9 cm)* of insul.	R 12
A single glazed window	R 0.9
A double glazed window	R 1.8
A triple glazed window	R 2.8

It is apparent that many times more heat is lost per square foot of window than per square foot of wall or ceiling.

APPROXIMATE EFFECTIVENESS OF VARIOUS WINDOW TREATMENTS IN A NORTHERN CLIMATE ON EAST AND WEST WINDOWS.

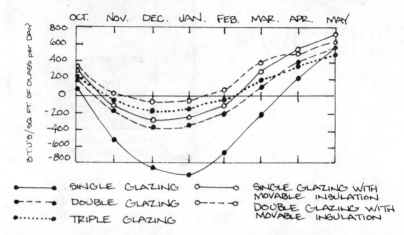

You can see from the chart that adding movable insulation to a single glazed window produces significant gains in energy savings, and for the amount invested can yield good returns. However, unless it is a well-sealed system, it may also increase problems with condensation since the difference in temperature between the room and the glass is increased. So be aware that condensation is a matter to be reckoned with.

STORM WINDOWS

Most experts recommend the addition of storm windows or double glazing at some point as part of your energy plan. Storm windows, while not perfect, do reduce the heat loss of windows by about 50% and they are always there and working—even when you are gone. They also reduce moisture problems caused by extremes of temperature between movable insulation and single glazing. You may choose to add movable insulation first, but it is wise to allow for the addition of storms or double glazing at a later date. As you can see from the chart below, the best combination appears to be double glazing plus movable insulation.

Outside storm windows cannot be considered decorative, and will not be treated in this book. But it is fair to say that inside storm windows do relate to the aesthetic aspects of our interiors. There are many types available: do it yourself versions of flexible vinyl fastened to windows or framework, less expensive styles of flexible or semi rigid plastic in frames, and sophisticated styles with glass in fixed or sliding aluminum frames colored to blend with your woodwork.

You may want to look at both outside and inside models before you make a final decision, particularly if your home has horizontal sliding aluminum frame windows. Advances in inside storm windows for this type of window are considerable and are worth investigating. Inside storm windows can also make it easier to get the tighter seal on the inside window—thus reducing condensation problems significantly.

The insulating value achieved by a window treatment can be greatly diminished if there are air leaks that allow heat or cold to escape around the edges. As a friend put it after we had toured my home discussing the kinds of things I was doing and hoped to do, "I never thought of it this way, but what you're trying to do is get a seal like around a refrigerator door." Now she really understood seals—no gaps or holes. And as she said, when she looks at window treatments now, she'll have a much better idea of what she wants to attain. "It means more than just hanging up a heavy drape."

Thus, once again, whatever you choose must be carefully installed, well sealed, and most importantly, used. R-11 insulating shutters are of no value if they remain open on very cold nights or days. Shading devices cannot cool your home if they are not in place on hot days. So once you are motivated to do something about window insulation, you must be motivated to activate the system regularly.

COMPARISON OF WINDOW TREATMENTS

REDUCTION OF	HEAT LOSS	HEAT GAIN
Type of Treatment over single glazing	% winter	% summer
Pinch Pleated Draperies		
Unsealed	6% or less	33%
All edges sealed	21-25%	—*
Roller Shade Std. Opaque vinyl		
Unsealed, ¼″ (6mm) clearance	24-31%	47-54%
Sealed edges	35%	50%+
Roller Shade Clear Mylar Reflective		
Unsealed	45%	10-15%
Sealed	55%	—*
Venetian Blind (Lt. Colored)		
Closed	6-7%	29%
Open at 45° angle	—*	18%
VERASOL Pleated Shade, med. color	49%	54%
Woven Wood, tightly packed yarns		
¼″ (6 mm) inside mount	33%**	—*
Roman Shade		
Medium colored inside mt., ¼″ (6mm)	20-25%	49%
Insulated, sealed edges	83%	—*
Shutters		
Louvered, wood	—*	—*
Rigid insulated, sealed	95%	—*

*Indicates I could not locate statistics for this item.
**Higher when shade is backed with reflective film.

NOTE: This chart is only to give an idea of the approximate effectiveness of different treatments. Results would vary with method of construction and materials used.

If you already have one of the treatments listed above and plan to keep it, look at ways to improve the mount or seal. If you want to further improve energy effectiveness, consider the addition of another layer, i.e. shade, shutter, etc.

ABOUT FABRICS

To be effective at saving energy fabrics used in window treatments should be

- Resistant to heat transfer
  Multiple layers, reflective surface, fibrous dimension creating air spaces, tightly woven

- Impervious to Air Flow and Moisture
  Tightly woven (i.e. nylon, polyester) or coated, vinyl, mylar, etc.
  **A plastic vapor barrier is advisable for high humidity rooms and cold northern climates. For moderate climates a tight layer of nylon or a coated fabric is often adequate.

- Sealed Tightly to Window

There are many readily available fabrics that can fit these criteria. If your current treatments do not, consider what might be added to the system or what changes are required to improve them. When decorating or redecorating consider these points when choosing fabrics. Don't overlook quilted fabrics of various types that have built-in insulating value because of the dead air spaces created by the filler material.

The increased interest in energy efficiency has spawned a number of new fabric products and new uses for some old ones—particularly those developed for the space program. Some add reflectance to bounce heat back into a room. Others are vapor barriers to prevent moisture from getting to the glass and condensing. Some are full of loft creating dead air spaces which are good insulators, and still others have combinations of these properties.

It is possible to use one or several layers of materials to help insulate window treatments. Your choices will no doubt be influenced by the amount of insulating you want or need, the finished look of the system, and what is available to you. To help solve the latter problem, you will find some mail order resources listed in the back of the book. Try your local resources, but if you have difficulty finding a specific product, these people may be of help.

While a single layer in shades or drapes may be effective at reducing heat loss (if edges are sealed properly), it is generally accepted that adding one or more layers to do a specific job can further increase the treatment's efficiency.

Every treatment varies due to the type of construction, window type, and method of installation. But it is safe to say that adding a layer of mylar in a treatment can improve its efficiency; adding a layer of needlepunch mylar or

Astrolar, etc. can improve it further, and Warm Window™ or comparable layers can create still more efficiency. There is logically a point beyond which the layers get too bulky, or the cost for savings achieved is out of proportion. Much of that depends on each person's situation and preferences.

Since you are not having testing done on each shade or window, just HOW effective a treatment is may be only an educated guess. But it can be a fairly good guess by comparing it to systems that we know have been tested and certified. As more research is documented, we will all be better educated on this subject.

NOTE: This chart is included here to show the diminishing return of higher R-values. The largest savings of energy for the money is usually achieved in the lower R-value range. It is true that the higher the R-value the more heat loss is reduced, but there is a point at which the cost of providing a higher R-value in a window treatment can't be recovered by the small amount of additional energy savings.

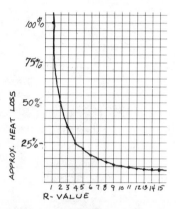

INSIDE STORM WINDOWS can be attractive and efficient. In addition they make it easier to get the tighter seal on the inside window.

Photo Courtesy of the MILAM Corporation

37

FABRICS AND MATERIALS USED FOR WINDOWS

Product	Manuf. or Distributor	Description and Uses	Reflects Radiant Heat	Vapor Barrier
Polyethylene	Various	Used as vapor barrier and in storm windows. 1-2 yr. life if exposed to sun. Transmits radiant energy.		X
Vinyl Film	Various	Vapor barrier in shades and in storm windows. Available in many weights. More expensive than polyethylene. Reduces infrared radiation. 5-6 yr. life in sun.		X
Mylar film	duPont Co. Madico Co.	Tough, thin, flexible film w/aluminized coating. Can be rolled without losing shiny appearance.	X	X
Astrolon	King-Seely Thermos Co.	Aluminum film between poly-ethylene films. Formerly call-ed Space Blanket. Astrolon III and VII are flame resistant.	X	X
Zero Perm	Aluminiseal Corp.	Alum. foil between ½ mil. mylar sheets.	X	X
Foylon 4413	Duracote Corp.	Thin film sheet w/alum. foil on one side for use in shades and liners.	X	X
Foylon 7001	Duracote Corp.	Lightweight alum. coated polyester fabric used as liners and in shades.	X	
Tyvek	duPont Co.	Sheet of very strong poly-olefin fabric w/ aluminum vacuum deposited on one side. Shades and liners.	X	X
Insalume®	John Boyle	Various combinations of fibers, films and foam combined with a micro-thin coating of aluminum on polyester film. Shades and liners.	Depends on the particular fabric.	
Needlepunch Mylar	Jen-Cel-Lite Corp.	Thin, reflective mylar film needlepunched with varying degrees of polyester fibers for insulation. 45" (115 cm), approx. $2.00 yd. Shades/liners/bedding.	X	

Product	Manuf. or Distributor	Description and Uses	Reflects Radiant Heat	Vapor Barrier
Astrolar	Astro-Temp Co., Inc. (Distr.)	Thin layer of Tyvek needle-punched with polyester fibers for warmth and insulation. 54″ (140 cm). Approx. $5.00 per yd.	X	
Needlepunch	Various	Polyester fibers in compact, lowbulk, relatively dense sheet. Endless uses in decorating/liners, shades, etc.		
Pellon Fleece	Pellon	Same		
ThermoLam® Plus	Stacy	Same		
Hollofil®	duPont Co.	Polyester insulating fiberfill or batting. Short, hollow fibers need to be stabilized with a backing. Multiple uses in decorating, bedding, quilted shades. About R-2 for 1″ (2,5 cm) thickness.		
Polar Guard®	Celanese	Continuous filament construction. Highly stable for use in bedding, shades. More loft for its weight than most synthetics. R-3.5 per 1″ (2,5 cm)		
Thinsulate®	3M	Highly insulative ultra-fine batting fibers. ¾″ (2 cm) thick, rated about R-4. More efficient and expensive than other batting types.		
Warm Window™	Warm Window	4-layer (needlepunch mylar, vinyl vapor barrier, needle-punch, thermal lining) channel quilted insulating fabric. Shades and mats. Tested to R-7.69. 45″ (115 cm) About $12.00 yd.	X	X
Double-face Foam-quilted (Placemat)	Various	Cotton on two sides with ¼″ (6mm) foam inner layer. Shades, mats, shutters. Approx. R-4 for two layers.		

In this chapter we'll look at options and ideas. Only you can make the ultimate decision about what you will do and what you can live with. The solutions for windows are not simple. Part of the confusion lies in the many types of windows, in the profusion of individual desires and preferences, and in costs and aesthetics. Part of it lies in the endless parade of products and techniques that are available. It is a good idea to clip ideas for your energy file. Try to be aware of new products, adapt ideas to your own situation and needs, and in general take comfort in the fact that you are concerned and you are doing something to conserve energy. (See Suggested Reading for other idea sources.)

NOTE: Beware of looking only at R-values, because R-values quoted with products are obtained in controlled laboratory situations. EVERY HOME AND EVERY WINDOW IS DIFFERENT. Keeping that in mind, use R-values generally as a guide.

Two excellent books deal solely with window insulation and reducing heating and cooling losses. You may want to buy or borrow a copy for a more in depth look at all aspects of windows. They are MOVABLE INSULATION by Wm. K. Langdon and THERMAL SHADES AND SHUTTERS by Wm. Shurcliff. (See Suggested Reading.)

WHAT CAN I DO? WHERE DO I START?

Analyze the windows throughout your home. Then, take it one room at a time. Start with north facing windows, or the largest windows (more heat loss occurs there), or with a large window or sliding glass door that is the source of discomforting drafts caused by thermosyphoning described on p. 49. If you live in a hot climate, start with those that cause the most problem with heat build-up. Think through the type of decor and mood you want. What can you do with your windows to achieve that look? What can you do to make an energy efficient treatment in the style you want? If the treatment pleases you as it is, what can you do to make it more efficient? How can you get the most efficiency for the dollars you will spend? As stated earlier in the book, some of our ideas and tastes may need to be reshaped for the sake of energy savings, but for the most part we can have the best of both worlds.

TIP: It is a good idea to look into what is available in your state in tax credits and financing for various movable insulation products. Utilities may offer low interest loans or other incentives for installing energy saving devices. Unfortunately, the Federal program is limited and specifically excludes window coverings at this time . . . though 40% renewable resources credit is applicable in some circumstances.

PROPER CLEARANCE HELPS SOLAR GAIN

During the winter, windows should be uncovered during the day when temperature is above 20° F. to allow the warmth of the sun to enter, resulting in direct heat gain through passive solar heating. This means that treatments should stack back on the wall and CLEAR THE GLASS (especially on south facing windows) to provide maximum area for sun to enter. Simply adjusting the placement of the treatment could increase your energy savings. For example, when we bought our home fully one-third of each window was covered when drapes were open because proper stackback had been overlooked.

Windows should be kept 'sparkling' clean in winter to allow as much natural warmth to enter as possible. Screens should not be left on windows in winter months, since even their fine mesh can reduce sunlight by as much as 20%, and free solar radiation through the windows by up to 40%.

Windows should be covered with shades, drapes, etc. in summer to reflect sun and prevent heat from entering and building up as the day progresses. Of course, maximum shading is achieved by awnings, screens, greenery or other OUTSIDE devices. The advantage being that heat starts to dissipate BEFORE it strikes and enters the house.

ROLLER SHADES

One of the very simplest and least expensive ways to improve efficiency of windows is to add a roller shade. I have made this suggestion to friends only to hear, "but I just HATE roller shades." There are two replies to that—one is to conceal the shade as much as possible with a box or flush cornice so it is hidden out of sight when not needed. But when you DO need it, there it is, just pull it down. The second answer lies in the belief that as the energy crisis increases, the appreciation of shades will also increase. The look of one type may not fit your decor, but there is sure to be another that will, and new types are being introduced all the time.

To achieve maximum efficiency both the method of mounting and the shade cloth must be carefully chosen. Close fitting or sealed edges and approximately a ¾" to 1" (2-2,5 cm) air space between shade and window are desirable. Heavy vinyl or reflective materials give more efficiency than plain fabrics. Additional layers can help increase efficiency.

You may make your own shades or select from commercial or custom types. You can laminate decorator fabrics to heavy vinyl or other shade to achieve a decorator look while saving energy. If you need to protect furnishings from fading or you don't want to impair a view, there are clear and reflective films (do-it-yourself or custom). Several shade manufacturers have introduced 'energy' shades, and more will undoubtedly follow. Graber calls theirs R-Value™ Insulating Shade, available in light filtering and room darkening style, and claims winter heat loss reduction of 40%; summer heat reduction of 80% if the shade is PROPERLY INSTALLED AND CORRECTLY USED.

You will face decisions about whether to make your own shades or purchase custom types, or perhaps some of both. Clip information for your file and be on the lookout for ideas that particularly suit your needs and decor.

ROLLER SHADE and EFFICIENCY INFORMATION

Here are some basic facts that are important if you plan to do-it-yourself. THE SHADE BOOK by Judy Lindahl, for everything you ever wanted to know about making and installing roller shades—and more (see p. 128) is suggested for further reading.

The Roller:

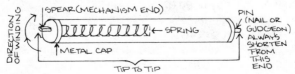

Mounting:

There are over half a dozen brackets which can be used. The two most common are the standard inside bracket and the outside bracket.

INSIDE BRACKETS

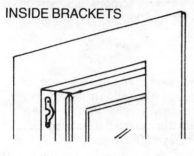

Used where there is enough depth inside a window frame for the roller. It is usually the most energy efficient because the side edges of the shade lie close to the window frame, helping seal the air flow. This type bracket may be reversed, that is, the spear is placed on the right frame and the round pin on the left. The difference in conventional roll and reverse roll is illustrated below.

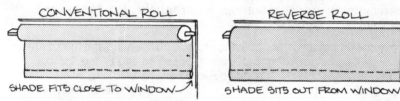

CONVENTIONAL ROLL

SHADE FITS CLOSE TO WINDOW

REVERSE ROLL

SHADE SITS OUT FROM WINDOW

ENERGY TIP

If your shade is pre-mounted or custom mounted it will be cut so the shade edges are 1/8-1/4" (3-6 mm) SHORTER than the roller. This is to allow clearance to prevent rubbing on brackets or window frame. However, with an inside mount, you can often get away with having the shade cloth cut the SAME AS, or LONGER THAN the roller barrel, especially if your window frames are flat and deep. The bracket must be small enough to fit inside the roll of the cloth.

SHADE CLOTH

BARREL

For double hung windows with recessed frames, the shade cloth can be cut extra narrow as shown, or some small blocks of wood can be set in the recess to build it up to create a flat opening for the bracket mount. Sometimes my shade cloth tends to roll back at the edges with this method, increasing the air gap. If this is a problem, you may need to consider some type of channel or filler strip to hold shade edges in line. (Illustrations show top view.)

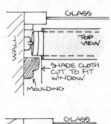

GLASS

TOP VIEW

SHADE CLOTH CUT TO FIT WINDOW

WALL

MOULDING

GLASS

FILLER BLOCK

BRACKET

MOULDING

WALL

OUTSIDE BRACKETS

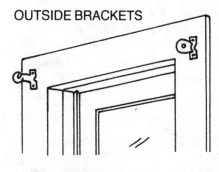

Mounted on trim or wall next to the window. Use when window is not deep enough for an inside bracket, for shades wider than window, to eliminate light streaks, or to give illusion of wider window. Generally, less efficient than inside brackets unless steps are taken to keep shade edges close to the wall. Expansion bolts are recommended for wall mount. Also available in reverse brackets.

If your shades are currently mounted on outside reverse brackets, you can make them more efficient by changing to a conventional mount.

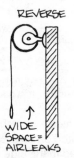

REVERSE

WIDE SPACE = AIRLEAKS

CONVENTIONAL

SMALL SPACE REDUCES AIRLEAK

Things to Remember if you make or mount your own shades:

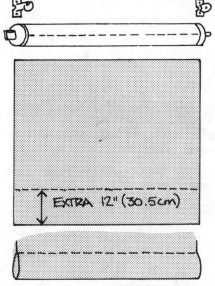

Brackets must be LEVEL.

Guideline for mounting shade.

Shade cloth must be cut SQUARE and mounted SQUARE.

Short staples or tape can be used for the mounting.

EXTRA 12" (30.5cm)

Cut shade 12″ *(30,5 cm)* longer than window opening.

Use a flat bottom edge. Stitch or glue a pocket for slat or rod.

See p. 128 to order THE SHADE BOOK:

SEALING SHADES

Many of the energy products on the market come with channels, tracks, or magnetic strips to seal the shades. It improves the efficiency of any shade when it is sealed. Vertical tracks can be made from aluminum, plastic, or wood strips fastened to the sides of the window frame. Flush or box cornices can help seal shades at the top.

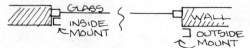

Insul-Shields (Patented)

These inside storm window kits have a 1" *(2,5 cm)* rigid plastic channel with a peel and stick mounting for application to a window frame. It is made for 5 mil clear lumar or reflective mylar shades which the company sells. I have experimented with the channels and find that they can be used on good quality vinyl and decorator shades. The channel sells for approximately 40¢ per linear foot and may be painted to blend with your decor. (See p. 127.)

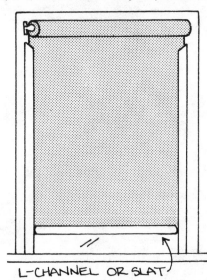

L-CHANNEL OR SLAT

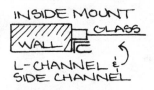

For inside mount the side channel is mounted on an L-channel which is applied to the side of the window frame.

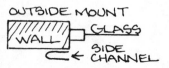

Position side channels so shade fits well into the slot, with about ⅛" *(3 mm)* clearance at the outer edge. The surface of the window frame should be clean and dry before channels are applied. Wiping the surface with rubbing alcohol before applying channels removes grease and aids in a tight bond.

When pulling shades always pull them in the center or with one hand at each side to keep them level. Do not grab only one side.

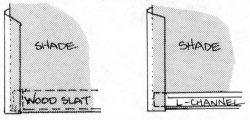

Even the rigid plastic channels designed for sliding doors can be used for shade systems. Peel and stick foam weatherstrip can be used to decrease the size of the channel if desired.

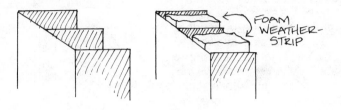

Magnetic Seals

Several systems use flexible self-stick magnetic tapes to create a seal. The magnetic tape is available in a variety of widths and thicknesses—the thinner the better for application to shades that must roll. Usually, however, the magnetic tape is applied to the window frame and a very thin flexible steel tape is applied to the edges of the shade itself. The tapes may be painted to blend with frame and room decor. Both types of tape are available by mail. (See Resources.)

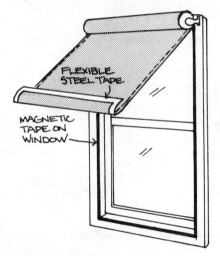

One thing that I like about the magnetic system is that it allows for different types of window treatments to be used on the same magnets, thus you can change decor and still maintain a good window system.
For example:
1. Transparent roll up shade
2. Reflective roll up shade
3. Decorator fabric shade
4. Roll up quilted shade
5. Roman shade
6. Window 'mats'
7. Inside storm window

DETAILS OF IDEAS FOR FINISHING BOTTOM OF SHADE:

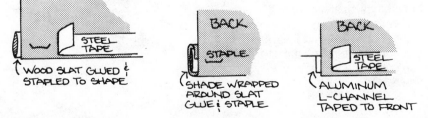

In his book MOVABLE INSULA-
TION, William Langdon suggests a
simple technique of using a magnetic tape on the sides of the window
frame and then sealing the shade by
setting a length of steel shelving on
top. You could paint the steel strip or
glue fabric, ribbon or trim down the
center of the channel. When shade
is raised, steel strips are stored on
the magnetic strips.

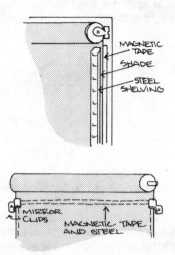

If there is enough clearance at the
top of the window, you may be able
to place a magnetic strip on the
frame and the shade to create the
top seal.

Another quick way to gain or improve a top seal on roller shades is to staple
or tape a strip of clear vinyl, lumar, insulating lining, needlepunch, etc. along
the top of the window casing so it rests on the shade as it rolls and unrolls. It
is also useful where shades of different thickness are interchanged seasonally, requiring brackets to be set lower for the thicker shade.

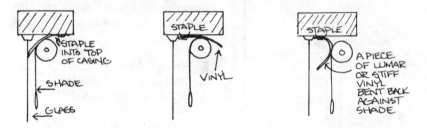

TWO SHADE SYSTEM

Take advantage of the benefits of layering and at the same time have two
shades that perform different functions. For example, one may be a fabric
laminated decorator shade, the
other a reflective fabric, or clear
shade that lets sun and heat in and
stops ultraviolet rays that fade your
furnishings. Just mount one shade
in reverse mount and one in conventional. For outside mount systems, a
box cornice helps the top seal and
can conceal both shades if
you desire.

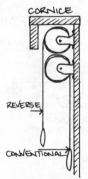

LAYERED SHADES

Another way to improve the efficiency of a shade is to add a layer of reflective backed cloth, such as Foylon, needlepunch mylar, or Astrolar®

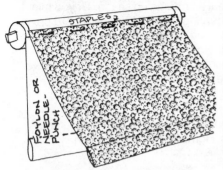

for both reflection and insulation. The latter two are thicker and would require more clearance for the roll of the shade. They both have a heat/cold reflective sheet (mylar or tyvek) needlepunched to fuzzy polyester fibers to give loft and insulation.

Staple the new layer so it rests behind your original shade. The two will roll together. If you decide to make the reflective layer a perma-

nent part of your shade by bonding it with fusible web or laminating with glue, read THE SHADE BOOK (see p. 128) for these techniques. However the loose layers work quite satisfactorily, and create added air space for better insulation.

ENERGY TIP If your original shade is narrow with air leaks at the sides, make the reflective layer wider so it touches the frame and creates a seal.

NOTE: Your old roller may not be strong enough to lift both layers of fabric. You may need to purchase a heavy duty roller from a shade shop.

If you do not have an outdoor shading device for summer heat control, and you want to cut the glare and heat of the sun while retaining privacy without losing viewing, consider fiberglass openwork screening (see Resources). This mesh is actually designed for outside installations, but makes fine shades inside the house, too. This is an alternative to the highly reflective types of shades. It is sometimes referred to as a Comfort Shade.

NOTE: Remember an outdoor shading device is seven times more effective than inside shading devices such as drapes, shades, etc., since the sun is actually stopped from entering the house.

CONCEALING A SHADE.

Some people are not bothered by a roller shade at the top (or bottom) of a window. Others can't seem to tolerate it. If you fall in the latter group, consider box or flush cornices or lambrequins to help trap air and to conceal the shades until you need them. (Construction details on pp. 79-84.)

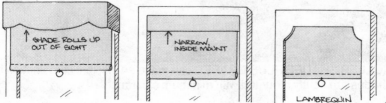

For example, you might install a narrow flush cornice from a board painted or stained to match your woodwork so it becomes part of the window itself—yet it conceals the energy saving shade. A narrow flush 'cornice' at the bottom of the window could conceal a bottoms up shade. Or you might use a ruffle, swag, or valance on a mounting board. I built cardboard box cornices for my daughters' rooms. They are padded and covered in fabric to match the bedspreads, attached by straight pins, and conceal both a venetian blind and a room darkening shade mounted behind it. I can lower either or both, or raise either completely out of sight. It works great!

COMBINE A SHADE

Shades can be added to other treatments to make them more efficient. A roller shade works with all treatments. Roman or other types can also be used.

Shade + draw draperies or tiebacks
Shade + venetian blinds
Shade + cafe curtains (alone they are NOT efficient)
Shade + folding screens
Shade + louver shutters

Photo Courtesy of James Seeman Studios, Wallcovering; A Div. of MASONITE Corp.

ROLLER SHADES PLUS DRAPES can make an efficient combination if shades are tightly mounted with minimum clearance.

Shade + ruffled tieback curtains
Shade + sheers and/or casements and drapes
Shade + shirred drapes or side panels
Shade + swags and cascades

DRAPERIES

The most common type of window treatment is the pinch pleated drapery.
Since drapes stand away from the wall, they are not sealed at top and
bottom and air leaks are inevitable.

Tests at the University of Georgia
showed that on cold nights air currents behind a drapery actually set
up their own thermosyphoning loop.
As air comes in contact with cold
glass it cools rapidly and drops, thus
pulling in more air at the top. In summer the open top allows trapped
heat to rise into the room.

Thus 'insulated' linings and drapery
fabrics really have little effect as
long as they remain open at top and
edges.

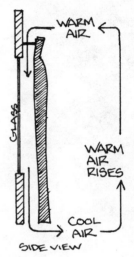

Improving the Efficiency of Draperies

ADD A SHADE

One of the simplest ways to get an immediate increase in efficiency is to add
a well mounted, preferably sealed, shade. While a roller shade may be the
easiest and most compatible with many treatments, Roman and other
shades can be effective, too.

NOTE: For those who want something that is the LEAST NOTICEABLE,
roller shades, which can be rolled high out of the way or shielded with a
narrow 'flush' cornice, or the Verosol® pleated shade which compresses to
½" (1,3 cm) for each 2 foot (61 cm) drop may be 'best bets'.

SEAL THE EDGES
Seal the Top
Sealing the top of the drapery is an important step in stopping air flow behind
the drape and increasing efficiency. This can be accomplished in a number
of ways.

Add a Cornice

A closed top cornice (or valance) stops air from flowing behind the drapery. Take heart in the fact that a cornice need not be a costly, heavy, unwieldy wood box. There are numerous tricks for making them light, attractive, easy to contruct and install. See the section on Cornices for directions.

Photo Courtesy of Waverly Fabrics, Designer: Barbara Egner

Try a Lambrequin

A lambrequin is basically a cornice with sides. Often the sides go clear to the floor, thus top and bottom seals are taken care of at the same time. Treatments with lambrequins are very eyecatching (they combine with drapes, shades, etc.) and certainly worthy of consideration.

Photo Courtesy of James Seeman Studios, Wallcovering; A Div. of MASONITE Corp.

Use a Ceiling Mount

Mounting the drapery rods on the ceiling stops air flow patterns and eliminates the need for a cornice. It will require longer drapes, however, so may not be the solution for your current drapery system.

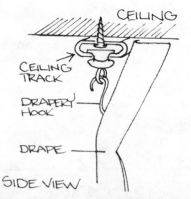

Photo Courtesy of Van Luit & Co., Photography: George R. Szanik

CEILING MOUNT creates an efficient installation. Even better when sides and bottom are sealed, too.

The Board System—Built-in Top Seal

This ingenious mount is used by one of the best custom drapery houses in Portland, Oregon. Developed by Jeff Goodell, it creates a 'ceiling mount' at the window that presents a smooth, clean look since no bare rod or brackets show when drapes are open. The board is stained or painted to blend with the woodwork or walls. You get a closed top system mounted at (or just above) window level—and no cornice needed!

In Goodell's system a channel is routed out of a board, holes are pre-drilled at an angle approximately every 18" *(46 cm)* for mounting. The board is stained or painted, then architectural type track (they use Kirsch #92000 Series) is mounted in the channel. The board is mounted at the window and sits on top of the window frame. Screws (2½" #8) go through the angled holes directly into the header beams above the window. Angle irons used under the outer ends of the board for additional support are hidden by the drapery when it is stacked back. The drape is brought around the ends of the board and secured to a plate available with the components. (Be sure to seal edges of drape to the wall.)

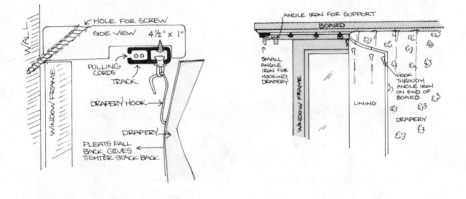

NOTE: This system is available with pinch pleat, roll fold, or knife pleat headings. One nice feature is that the roll and knife styles can be ordered with a butted closing. This makes sealing the center of the drapery much easier—especially with magnetic strips.

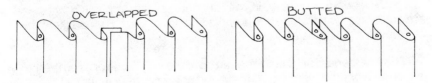

A tighter seal might be achieved by some of the suggested variations that follow:

1. Instead of recessing the entire rod, notch the front of the board to accept the rod at the front edge. In this technique the drapery is hooked so it conceals the front of the board when closed, or it may be placed just below the rod and in a regular ceiling mount.

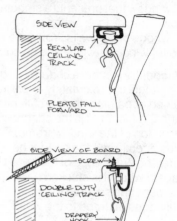

2. Drape may be hung high to conceal board, or lower as in regular ceiling mount, but this must be determined early as it affects the length of the drapery.

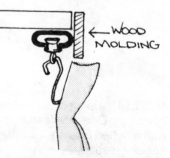

3. Instead of notching the board, mount track on the front edge. Saves time and expense, though the track shows.

Or conceal the track by adding a narrow piece of wood molding to the front edge of the board.

Top Gaskets

Several people are working on a gasket that will seal the top of the drapery to a cornice board or to the wall. They are not available at this time, but these are products to watch. One that is under testing is called "Fluff Gasket®" by D. Russell Associates of Jacksonville, Fla.

NOTE: A cardboard or fabric 'filler' can be made to fit inside or sit on the top of a curtain or drapery rod to 'seal' the top of your current treatment.

Seal the Sides
Drapery edges should be fastened to the wall. This can be accomplished in a number of ways.
1. Fasten directly to the wall with nylon fastener (Velcro, Gripper Strip, etc.)
2. Tack edges directly to the wall
3. Hold edges with magnetic strips (may be painted to match wall)
4. Pull taut with hooks
5. Clamp at sides with board clamps.

Seal the Center
For maximum effect drapes should be sealed at center. They may be fastened with snaps (nylon clear snaps are nearly invisible), nylon fastener tape, magnetic strips, or clips. Unfortunately, no one has come up with a really easy, inconspicuous seal . . . yet.

But tests show the need for the seal. Drapes sealed at center showed a 21% reduction of heat loss; without a center seal it was only 10%.

As mentioned earlier, some types of drapery hardware offer a choice of overlap or butt closures. The butt system is easiest to seal.

NOTE: An alternative to sealing the drapery fabric itself might be to add a drapery liner and place seals on those edges. An exception to sealing edges would be when a tightly fitted treatment made from dark-colored heat absorbing fabric is exposed to direct, prolonged sunlight and high temperatures. It could accumulate enough heat to crack or even shatter glass.

Seal the Bottom
This may be the hardest seal to achieve. Drapes should touch the sill, floor, or carpet. They should be weighted or may need to be held down to prevent billowing. Weights in the hem, long, skinny tubes of sand, beans, etc. inserted in hems or laid on top of hems, boards that clamp drapes to the wall, small troughs to hold the drapery have all been used. It remains for you to decide what works best and appeals to your eye. Hopefully someone will give us a good solution to this problem that is simple and attractive, too. I'll be only too glad to print it when it is found.

DRAPERY LINERS

Adding a liner behind your drapery can further aid in reduction of heat loss (or gain), but again—it should be sealed or be part of a sealed system. Some may add a liner so they can seal it at sides, center and bottom without having to make changes on the drapery itself.

The choices for liners are plentiful. Some types are available from mail order catalogs (Sears, Penneys). There are several commercially available such as Wind N Sun Shields of Melbourne, Fla., which are reflective silver on one side and white vinyl on the other. They are made to be reversed—silver side in for winter, out for summer. Another is the Warm-In Drapery Liner from Conservation Concepts Ltd., Stratton, VT. It uses a layer of bubble polyethylene between two layers of cotton, magnetic seals on leading edges.

Many people are making their own simple and inexpensive liners from needlepunch mylar, Astrolar, Astrolon, Foylon, and other reflective materials. Basically you overlap strips and stitch, glue, or fuse—depending on the material, creating enough length and width to allow for a good seal. Eyelets or buttonholes are used along the top edge so the liner is hung in place behind an existing drapery (on same hooks) or on its own rod.

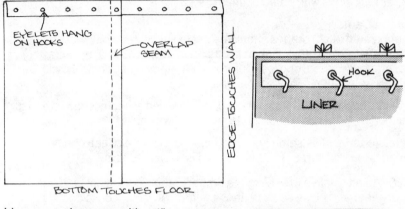

Liners may be sewn with a 1" *(2,5 cm)* tuck stitched midway between eyelets. This increases fullness and helps them stack more neatly. (Allow for tucks when measuring.)

Eyelets should be small, ⅛" *(3 mm)*. Large grommets interfere with stacking when drapes are opened. Top edge should be folded once or left unfolded and reinforced if not strong enough to hold the weight of the liner.

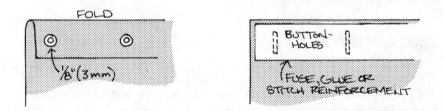

Most of these fabrics need no seam or edge finish, so construction is very simple. If you need a vapor barrier, consider that when choosing a product or add a layer of thin plastic just beneath the drapery fabric.

DRAPERY LAYERS

Fabric or other layers can help create air spaces and insulation to improve efficiency of drapery systems. (For example, linings or sheers may be mounted separately.) But all layers need to be sealed for best effect.

ROMAN SHADES

Roman shades are particularly attractive and suited to improving energy efficiency. They have a built-in top seal, relatively easy to seal edges, look well alone or in combination with other treatments, and the efficiency of basic shades can easily be improved.

The basic shade is flat when down. When cords strung through rings and screw eyes or pulleys are pulled, the shade falls into pleats.

Unlike a roller shade, the excess fabric does not disappear when the shade is raised. The shade must be constructed and mounted square to hang evenly.

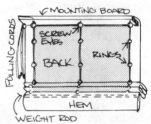

FABRICS

For energy efficiency choose medium weight, firmly woven fabrics; avoid loose, open weaves. Select a white or off-white lining. Look for thermal or stain and mildew resistant treatment. If room darkening is important, choose blackout lining, though small pin holes of light may show through where rings are sewn.

To increase the energy efficiency of a shade one or more of the following can be included in the construction. (In general they are listed from least to most efficient.) Also see chart on pp. 38-39.

- Polyethylene or vinyl film sheeting. Primarily for vapor barrier.
- Polyester batting, quilt batting, such as Polar Guard, Hollofil, etc. Plain needlepunch.
- Mylar, Astrolon, or other films or coated vinyl to help reflect heat and cold and provide a vapor barrier.
- Foylon or other lightweight reflective fabrics to reflect heat and cold. Fabrics are not vapor barriers.
- Needlepunch mylar or Astrolar provides air spaces and reflectance, but is not a vapor barrier.
- Thinsulate ® by 3M, very high in insulating value for amount of bulk.
- Warm Window™ 4-layer channel quilted insulating fabric.

MOUNTING VARIATIONS

How you mount your shade influences other measurements, so make that decision early. A 1″ × 2″ (2,5 × 5 cm) board is usually used for mounting. This size is not sacred, however.

Inside Mount
The shade fits entirely within the opening. Accuracy in construction and mounting are critical, since the opening defines and outlines the shade. For energy savings, edges should touch or be not less than ⅛″ (3 mm) from frame. Better yet, they should be sealed.

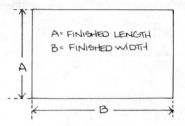

Cut mounting board to fit inside the opening. Fasten by screws through board into window frame, or by fastening angle irons to the under-side of the window frame. Mount angle irons toward the back of the board so they don't get in the way of screw eyes or pulleys.

Outside Mount
The shade is installed above the opening on the frame, wall or ceiling. Stacked pleats can clear the frame, taking advantage of solar heat in winter. Edges usually overlap the frame by ¾″ (2 cm) or more.

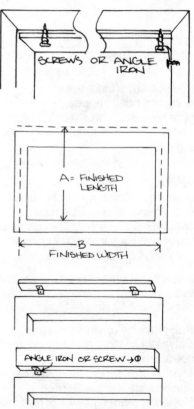

Mounting board is placed on angle irons as illustrated.

To get a tighter fit of the shade, try turning the board on edge or use a 1″ × 1″ (2,5 cm × 2,5 cm).

NOTE: Handles of sliding glass doors may protrude enough to require modification of the handle, or widening the shade beyond the handle or building a frame extension around the door. It is also possible to mount a board at the center of the patio door, so two shades can be constructed rather than one wide one. A common cornice can unify the treatment.

Hybrid Mount

The board fits inside the frame but the shade is made wider, about ¾″ *(2 cm)*, on each side so it rests on the frame, creating a tighter seal. The bottom edge can rest on sill, or flat against wall.

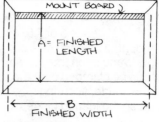

HEM DEPTH AND RING PLACEMENT

Another decision that affects finished measurements of the shade is hem depth. The standard hem depth on a Roman shade is one half the distance between rows or rings. For example, if rings are 6″ *(15 cm)* apart, the hem would be 3″ *(7,5 cm)* deep. Thus when the shade is raised, the folds are protected from the sun by the hem.

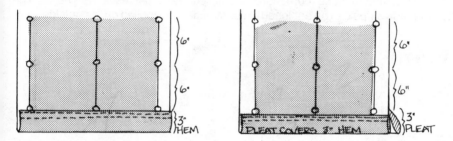

If you desire a band of hem to show when the shade is raised, the hem must be made deeper.

NOTE: If you do not plan to add a cornice or valance you may wish to add a row of rings just below or near the mounting board. This holds the shade in and keeps it from 'poking out' at the top and revealing the mounting board when the shade is pulled. You may wish to sew the rings on, then decide whether or not you need them when you string the shade.

EDGE SEALS

A well fitted Roman shade can give an energy savings of around 20% to 25%. With tight edge seals and layers of insulating fabrics, that can be improved to as high as 83%.

FRICTION FIT

A simple seal is achieved by making the shade a couple of inches wider than the opening and tucking the excess in to touch the frame when shade is down. Small Velcro tabs, hooks, or pieces of flexible magnetic tape can be used to secure the edges in a taut position.

BOARD CLAMPS

1" × 2" or 1" × 3" *(2,5 × 5 or 7,5 cm)* board is mounted on each side of the window frame or on the wall so that they can be clamped over the edges of the shade, securing it tightly. Use spring loaded hinges.

MAGNETIC SEAL

Strips of flexible magnetic tape can be applied to window frame or wall and to edges of a Roman shade to form a tight seal. (Flexible steel tapes can also be used to mate with a magnetic strip.) Both steel and magnetic tapes can be painted to make them more inconspicuous or rust resistant. The shade tape strips can be enclosed in construction, or applied on the outside.

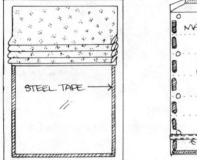

Standard Method

This is my favorite method. It is fast and accurate because fabric is prepared on work surface first, then lining is positioned on the face fabric. A minimum of handling and pressing is required. Though the faced hem technique takes more time, it is an attractive finish, since only lining fabric shows on the outside of the house. (Side hems are concealed by window casing.)

Fabric may need to be seamed to create width. Seam one full width in center with equal strips at sides, matching design where needed. Plan rings to fall behind seams if possible.

PART WIDTH	FULL WIDTH	PART WIDTH

MEASURING

Width = Finished width plus 3" *(7,5 cm)*. Add for seam allowances if fabric must be pieced for width.
Length = Finished length plus 3" *(7,5 cm)*
Lining = Finished width and finished length + 3" *(7,5 cm)*
Facing Strip = 5" *(12,5 cm)* deep × finished width + 2" *(5cm)*

NOTE: If adding more layers, cut them same as lining.

1. Cut, seam, and press shade fabric—keeping it square. If fabric ravels easily, zig-zag side edges, turn under ¼" *(6 mm)*, or treat with glue. Lay fabric right side down on cutting board or work surface. Square fabric if needed. Measure and mark finished width. Turn excess in at sides and press in equal hems.

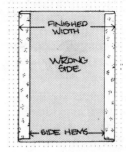

NOTE: The fabric was cut 3" *(7,5 cm)* wider to allow for 1½" *(3,8 cm)* side hems. This may change slightly due to zig-zagging, turn of cloth, steam shrinkage or handling of fabric.

2. Lay insulating layers (if used) on top of shade fabric and press smoothly in place. Mark width using shade fabric as guide. Cut to fit. Slip edges under the side hems. Add lining last. Pin the shade and lining together in a few places. Do not pin if you have included a vapor barrier. Use clothespins or clips around the edges.

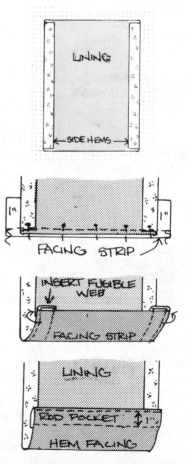

3. Slip facing strip under shade. Center and pin even with bottom edge, leaving 1" *(2,5 cm)* extending at sides. Stitch a ½" *(1,3 cm)* seam allowance along bottom edge.

   Smooth and press facing strip to wrong side. Fold and press side extensions in so they do not show from right side. Insert a strip of fusible web between the facing layers. Fuse.

4. Turn and press top edge of facing strip down to make a 3" *(7,5 cm)* hem. Stitch along top edge, then again 1" *(2,5 cm)* down to form rod pocket.

NOTE: If desired, stitch hem top, then stitch rod pocket 1" *(2,5 cm)* from BOTTOM edge.

5. Realign shade on cutting surface, lining side up. Mark ring locations—keeping rows even and parallel. Place first row at the top of the weight bar and approx. 1" (2,5 cm) in from side edges so side hems are held in place by rings.

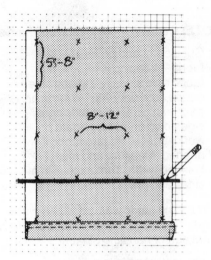

To speed marking and keep it accurate, use a long ruler or aluminum bar to lay across the shade. Draw very lightly with pencil or water soluble fabric marking pen. Mark all ring locations.

Vertical rows are usually 8" (20,5 cm) to 12" (30,5 cm) apart, horizontal rows are 5" (12,5 cm) to 8" (20,5 cm) with 6" (15 cm) being the general spacing.

NOTE: If you increase the distance between vertical rings, be sure to increase the hem depth half that amount.

6. Rings can be sewn by hand, but zig-zag button stitch on the sewing machine is faster. After a ring is secured with 8-10 stitches, lock the stitches by allowing the needle to penetrate the same spot for a few times. Move on to the next ring without cutting the threads. Sew as many rings as practical before you stop. Clip threads with a gentle touch so you don't pull out any stitches. Reinforce bottom row of rings; they carry the weight to the shade.

For some fabrics and especially on thicker shades, insert a corsage pin through fabric under the ring. Stitch over pin and ring to create a space or shank. Remove the pin. This eliminates a pull or pucker caused by tight stitches.

HINT: When sewing by hand you may wish to change thread color for different colors in the fabric. For this I thread several needles, each with the appropriate color. As I need to change color I have the needle all ready. OR use clear nylon thread for hand or machine sewing. Thread should be resistant to sunlight (Coats and Clark Crystal). Watch the pressing temperature; some threads are very heat sensitive.

7. Insert a ⅜" (1 cm) solid metal rod weight bar or ⅛" (3 mm) × ¾" (2 cm) flat bar (flat rod) in rod pocket. Rods are available in hardware stores, drapery shops, home improvement centers, and from Iron Works (see yellow pages). The bar should be painted or treated to resist rusting and cut ½" (1,3 cm) narrower than finished width.

Paint or wrap mounting board with lining fabric, if desired. Fusing or gluing fabric to board allows screw eyes to go in without pulling and twisting the fabric.

Position screw eyes in mounting board above each row of rings and slightly toward front edge. You may need one extra eye to help distribute the strain of the pulling cords. (See illus.) Using an awl or pre-drilling the holes reduces chances of splitting the board.

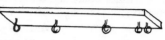

HINT: If the shade is very wide or very long, small pulleys or roller brackets (from drapery supply) can be used in place of screw eyes, to save wear and tear on cords.

Staple or tack the shade in place on the top of the mounting board.

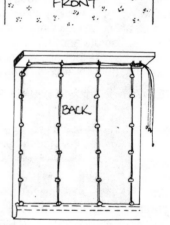

8. String the shade. Cut lengths of non-stretchy cord, one for each row of rings. Each will be a different length, but must go up shade and across top of window with excess at side for pulling.

9. Tie cords securely to bottom ring, and dab a bit of glue on the knot. Thread cords through rings and screw eyes. Final adjusting of cords will be done with shade in the window.

NOTE: Screw eyes at end where all cords come through must be large enough so cords don't bind up when pulled.

10. Mount shade in window. Adjust cord tension so it is equal on all cords. Then if desired, tie a knot below screw eyes when shade is DOWN. Check again to be sure tension is equal, then dab glue on knot to hold cords without slipping. Braid cords together below the knot and add a weighted drapery pull or tie another knot to hold cords.

Mount awning cleat on operating side to wind off cords when shade is pulled, or consider a lock pulley on mount board which allows the cords to be pulled and locked into any position (much like a venetian blind or woven wood).

Insulated Roman Shade (with magnetic seal)

There have been many plans and directions developed for insulating Roman Shades. If directions are followed carefully, they are very effective at conserving energy usually lost through the windows. Unfortunately, they are often rather bulky and untidy looking. One of the most attractive insulating shades that I have seen was developed in Seattle by Warm Window. Their shade utilizes the Warm Window™ insulated fabric (patent pending) which contains four layers (see chart p. 39) channel quilted together. You add your own choice of decorater fabric for the front. The fabric has gained rapid acceptance by do-it-yourselfers because the channel stitching helps reduce bulk, holds the layers in place so they don't shift, and serves as the location for the horizontal ring placement thus saving a tremendous amount of time and energy.

The following directions refer to Warm Window™ four layer insulating fabric (see p. 127.) You could use your own inner layers of materials if preferred. Notations indicate where a special change must be made if you use your own. The Warm Window™ shade utilizes a magnetic seal system which gives a clean, crisp look when shade is raised or lowered. You could, however, substitute another edge seal (friction fit, board clamp, etc.). This will cause shade to look slightly more bulky when raised, but will not change its insulating performance as long as seals are tight.

NOTE: Warm Window™ is run horizontally so the 8″ *(20,5 cm)* channels form the pleat locations.

Determine type of Mount (see p. 58.) and type of edge seals since these decisions influence finished dimensions.

MEASURING
Decorative Fabric:
    Width = Finished width plus 3″ *(7,5 cm)* (for side hems)
    Length = Finished length plus 8″ *(20,5 cm)* (3″ *(7,5 cm)* for mounting
        ease, 5″ *(12,5 cm)* for hem)
Warm Window™ (or interior layers)
    Width = Finished Width of shade
    Length = Finished length plus 3″ *(7,5 cm)* CUT FABRIC SO A 4″ *(10 cm)*
    CHANNEL FALLS AT BOTTOM OF THE SHADE.

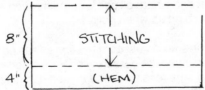

CONSTRUCTION—READ COMPLETELY BEFORE STARTING SHADE.

1. Cut, seam and press shade fabric—keeping fabric square and matching design as needed.

2. Prepare Warm Window™ or interior insulating layers, splicing where needed for length or width.

Warm Window™ is run HORIZONTALLY (called railroading). To seam fabric place lining sides together with two rows of channel stitching resting on top of each other. Baste and check for accuracy. Then stitch through the channel stitching with 8-10 stitches per inch *(2,5 cm)*. Trim and grade bulk from seam allowances.

Fold the nearer seam allowance down with your thumb and trim the other by holding the scissors flat to the fabric, which will cut the layers in a staggered fashion (grading). Cut about ⅛" *(3 mm)* from the stitching. Turn fabric around and repeat on remaining seam allowance. Press seam with fingers.

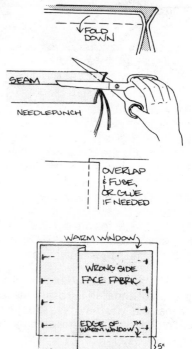

To splice layers of standard materials, overlap and fuse or glue edges, depending on the particular material. Seam lining fabric in standard way to create width.

3. Place right sides of fabric and lining together. Match top and side edges evenly. (Shade fabric will be larger.) Pin side edges.

4. Stitch ½" *(1,3 cm)* side seams. At this point you may turn the shade inside out to be sure width and length are correct. Turn extra bottom fabric up and pin in place. Recheck shade and window measurements.

FOR HYBRID MOUNT with ¾" *(2 cm)* overlap on frame: Place a pin on each side to mark finished top length. (Be sure pins are even.) Reach inside shade and mark pin location. Remove pins and turn shade wrong side out again.

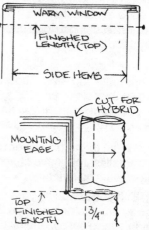

Zig-zag or overcast the fabric edges, catching all layers. FOR HYBRID MOUNT draw a line from side edge ¾" *(2 cm)* long, then draw it vertically to the top edge of the shade. Cut along this line. Repeat on other side.

5. Place a pin at each channel stitching location. This will aid in accurate magnet placement.

6. Mark magnetic strips into 3½" *(9 cm)* lengths. With permanent marker or pencil draw an arrow on each piece. Cut sections apart, then nip corners to remove sharp points.

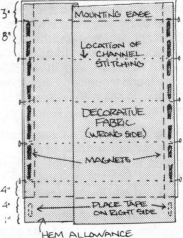

7. Remove paper backing from the magnetic strips and expose the adhesive. Place two strips between pins marking the channel stitching. Be sure arrows on magnetic strips point in the same direction. No strips in mounting ease and none on last 4" *(10cm)* of Warm Window. The bottom strips are cut 2½" long and are placed on the RIGHT side of the fabric seam allowance.

NOTE: Because window lengths fall in different locations, if possible have a row of rings fall just below the mounting board (see Note p.59). If this is not possible, you may have to adjust size of top pleat, or use a ⅝" *(1,5 cm)* mounting board. The narrower board is less noticeable. Or consider a cornice at the top.

8. Turn the shade right side out and smooth edges. Press with a cool iron. Fold the bottom up to form 4" *(10 cm)* hem. Add magnetic strip across bottom (optional) on wrong side of decorating fabric.

Taper sides slightly so they don't show on front side. Stitch close to top edge of hem, then 1" *(2,5 cm)* from first stitching to form pocket for weight rod or bar.

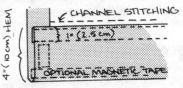

9. Mark the locations for rings. Each horizontal row is placed on the channel stitching lines. About 8"-12" *(20,5 to 30,5 cm)* apart. Place outer rows so they clear the window frame and magnetic tape—about 1½" *(3,8 cm)* from edge. (If you are not using Warm Window fabric, see directions for Standard Shade, steps 5 and 6.)

Place a pin through all layers at each ring location taking care to pin horizontally through the channel stitching. Sew rings by hand or zig-zag button stitch on machine.

NOTE: If you are using your own fabric layers, it may be advisable to sew rings by hand to help reduce the shifting of layers. If you use the machine, handle shade gently, and be sure each ring point is pinned.

10. Cut the weight rod to fit easily inside window opening. Smooth the cut ends or wrap with tape. Insert in rod pocket and tack ends of opening closed.

11. Re-read mounting information and step 7 under Standard Shade. Place screw eyes in mounting board; mount shade if inside or outside mount. (Trim extra fabric from top edge, if needed.)

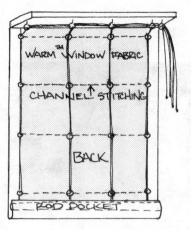

FOR HYBRID MOUNT: Front corners must be notched so mounting ease fits inside window, but shade edges extend over frame.

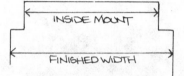

Cut decorative fabric where indicated below. Fold side hem extension down once, then again and tack in place on back side. Zig-zag or whip raw edge in mounting ease. (This forms mounting notches.) Mount on board. Trim excess length from mounting ease if needed.

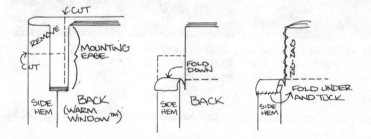

12. String the shade and add cleat or pulley. See steps 8 through 10 on standard method.

13. Mount the peel and stick magnetic tape on the wall or frame where the shade overlaps. Magnetic tape may be painted with enamel or a latex, if desired.

   To raise the shade release the seal at bottom edge (a small pull tab is helpful to protect the lower edge of the shade). Then pull cords. The pleats may need some hand shaping until they get a memory of their own.

Photo Courtesy of Warm Window

WARM WINDOW™ Insulating Fabric is used to create energy efficient Roman Shades for patio doors and side windows. Note the wall mount which allows stack back to clear the doors.

OVERLAPPING MAGNETIC SEAL

Here's a bright idea that works! For patio doors or wide windows place shades in an overlapping position with the enclosed magnet strips placed so they bond to each other when shade is lowered. A common cornice or valance unifies the treatment. The only drawback is that when both are raised, they won't line up evenly because of the overlap technique.

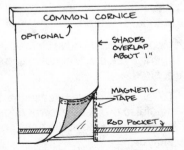

68

IMPROVING ROMAN SHADE EFFICIENCY

If you already own Roman shades and do not wish to part with them, try analyzing the things you could do to create a tighter mount and make them more efficient.

INSIDE MOUNT SHADES

1. Add side channels for edges to fit inside, or a molding extension for shade to rest against. OR—

TOP VIEW

U-CHANNEL

MOULDING EXTENSIONS

2. Add wood filler strips inside edge of window opening. Put peel and stick magnetic tape on filler strips and on back of shade edges (or use steel tapes) to create a magnetic seal.

OUTSIDE MOUNT

In the standard outside mount the shade sits out from the wall the depth of the mounting board.

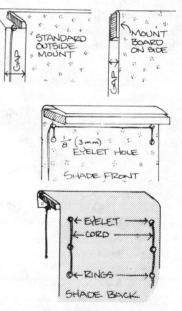

STANDARD OUTSIDE MOUNT

MOUNT BOARD ON SIDE

GAP

GAP

$\frac{1}{8}''$ (3 mm) EYELET HOLE

SHADE FRONT

EYELET

CORD

RINGS

SHADE BACK

1. Change the mounting board to a side installation. Add board clamps to shade edges if desired. OR—

2. Remove the shade from the mounting board and add ⅛" (3 mm) eyelets or tiny buttonholes at top of row of rings, just below the board. Staple shade to fall on back of board. Restring; add valance or cornice. Add magnetic seals or board clamps, if desired. OR—

3. Change shade to a Hybrid Mount. Re-measure finished shade length (shade will now fit inside top of window frame). Mark finished top length

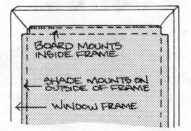

BOARD MOUNTS INSIDE FRAME

SHADE MOUNTS ON OUTSIDE OF FRAME

WINDOW FRAME

and inside mount line on back of shade. Cut from top edge to top finished length line, along inside mount line. Trim tab length then fold it under and tack to back of shade. Zig-zag or whip the raw edge of the mounting ease. Re-mount shade inside window.

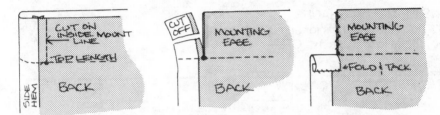

Add a Shade

If your Roman shade has a wide gap problem, or is of a decorative type that cannot be easily sealed, you may need to add a roller shade behind it to give added energy efficiency and create a layered treatment. Or if you have a favorite shade style such as cloud, balloon, tucks and eyelets that is not efficient that you want to use in your decorating scheme, plan to combine a roller shade or other treatment with it to achieve energy savings.

TIP: If some condensation does collect on windows, check seals. If it still occurs try placing a strip of stick-on open-cell foam weatherstripping about 1" *(2,5 cm)* from bottom of window. Water will be absorbed by the foam and can evaporate before damaging window frames.

You may also want to paint window frames with a low permeability (vapor barrier) paint as a basecoat—then latex or enamel to protect the framework.

INSUL TRAC (Pat. Pend.)

A new window track system from Plum Industries of Delta, Ohio, has potential for different types of windows since it can be mounted bottom up, top down, side to side, or on skylights. The white or brown vinyl tracks are mounted at the window, snap sliders are slipped onto the channels and then snapped to the edge of your decorator fabric to which a special snap tape has been sewn.

It compresses to 1½" *(3,8 cm)* per 1 foot *(30,5 cm)* of window. For south facing windows, which need to be completely uncovered to take advantage of solar gain in winter, a flush wall mount might be advisable so stackback clears the glass area. Fabrics can be changed seasonally or as desired simply by snapping preferred layers on and off.

ROLL UP SHADES

A variation on a roller shade is the Coach Shade (see THE SHADE BOOK by Judy Lindahl) that rolls up from the bottom. These shades may be rigged on pull-up cords—or can be rolled up by hand and fastened at

the top with straps or ties. If the latter method is chosen, you must be able to reach the top of the shade easily, or you may not activate the shade as often as you should. An advantage of this type of shade is that in the outside mount it fits close to the frame, creating a rather good seal. A better edge seal can be obtained with board clamps or magnetic seals. It can also be combined with other treatments for the layered effect.

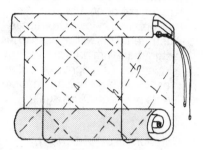

The insulating value of the shade can be increased by using a quilted fabric such as foam filled placemat fabric (usually comes with design on both sides, a factor in outside appearance) or several layers of insulating material. You might, for example, place a layer of mylar or Foylon between fabric and lining for reflective value. Batting or needlepunch contributes to insulating value, but also adds adds bulk. If you don't want to see the roll of fabric when the shade is up—make a fabric valance or simple cardboard box cornice.

MEASURING

Determine whether you will use an inside or outside mount for your shade.
Length = Finished length + 4" *(10 cm)*
Width = Finished width + 1" *(2,5 cm)*
Examples of layer combinations:

1. Carefully cut, seam and press shade and lining fabric, keeping it square. Prepare any insulating layers according to the nature of the materials.

Join fabrics by placing right sides of lining and decorative fabrics together and adding insulating layers as illustrated above. Stitch together with a ½" *(1,3 cm)* seam allowance around three sides, leaving top open. Leave a 1" *(2,5 cm)* opening at lower corner as illustrated. This will be used to insert weight bar. Trim bulk from seam allowance. Turn right side out and press. Re-check finished measurements of shade. Turn again.

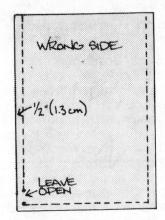

2. Cut a length of ⅛" *(3 mm)* by ⅝" *(1,5 cm)* or ¾" *(1,3 cm)* flat bar so it is ½" *(1,3 cm)* less than finished shade width. Paint or treat the bar to prevent rusting.

3. Stitch across the bottom edge of the shade to form a pocket for the bar. Insert bar and tack pocket closed.

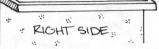

4. Staple shade to mounting board so fabric hangs down the back side of the board and bottom edge makes contact with sill or wall.

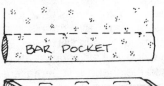

5. Anchor pulling cords securely to the back of the board. Side cords should be about 2" *(5 cm)* from edge of shade. Another cord at center may be needed with wider shades. Mount screw eyes on bottom of board in front of cord locations. Cords should be 3 times length of shade plus width.

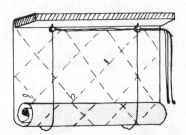

6. Prepare valance. Cut lining and fabric 10" *(25,5 cm)* deep by width of shade + 1" *(2,5 cm)*. Lay fabrics right sides together and stitch a ½" *(1,3 cm)* seam allowance around sides and bottom. Trim corners, turn and press. Staple to top of board so it falls forward and conceals screw eyes.

NOTE: The valance may be made to wrap around ends of board (for outside mount). It may be made deeper if needed to cover rolled up shade. You may want to make the shade, roll it, then measure for valance depth.

7. Mount shade in window. Secure cords with awning cleat or lock pulleys.

NOTE: For an optional outside mount— place the board on edge and screw directly through the board into the window frame or wall. The valance does not extend as far outward, but it will lie against the rolled up shade.

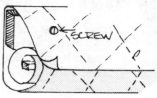

THERMAL SHADE™

Reflections of Milford, N.H. has available a custom made shade which is called the Thermal Shade™. It is made of an off-white five layer sonic quilted fabric and has magnetic Flex Seal™ edge seals to improve its insulating value. Cords are strung on a lock pulley system. They will also bond the customer's own fabric to the shade on special order.

VEROSOL® SHADES

These pleated sunscreen shades, imported from Europe, are not inexpensive (watch for sales to keep the cost down), but they are worth mentioning for a couple of reasons. When pulled up they compress to ½" *(1,3 cm)* for each 2 feet *(61 cm)* of length, you can see through them when they are lowered, and they have a reflective back coating which is helpful for reflecting summer sun and retaining heat in winter. They are more efficient than venetian blinds and are also available in bottoms up and skylight installation. New opaque fabrics are available if privacy is more important than view.

WOVEN WOODS

Woven woods are popular with many people for their warm, unfussy look. Their efficiency is related to the density of the yarns, the tighter the yarns the better, and the method of mounting—the tighter the better. Some companies are beginning to add a clear film to the back side which fills the spaces and increases efficiency. Light colors reflect more summer sun than darker tones.

Woven woods can be combined with other treatments to create layers and more efficiency. Even a roller shade behind the woven woods can help insulate and reflect more heat. So if you have this type of treatment, or are contemplating it—analyze the efficiency and how you can achieve your goals.

VENETIAN BLINDS

Venetian blinds are most effective for controlling view, privacy, and light. Due to openings between slats they reduce winter heat loss by only about 6-7%, and summer heat by 29%. Some types are aluminized on one side to increase their performance. Their efficiency can be improved by using them as part of a layered window system. Perhaps someone will develop a truly efficient venetian blind. It is not an impossibility, and would surely please those who love this window treatment.

Photo Courtesy of Ethan Allen

VENETIAN BLINDS become more efficient when layered with tighter treatments like cornices and drapes, shades, etc.

WINDOW MATS (For Home or Van)

Simple window-size mats can be created with layers of fabric (quilted fabrics work great), needlepunch (with or without mylar or tyvek) vapor barrier and lining. Magnetic or steel tape is applied to the edges of the mat, either on the outside (easier) or enclosed in the seam. Another strip is applied to the window frame or perimeter. The mat is popped in place to insulate and easily removed and rolled or hung for storage.

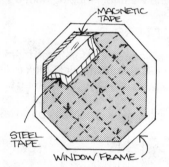

They are great for:
- North windows left covered a lot
- Odd-shaped windows
- Vans with energy-wasting windows
- Air conditioner covers
- Fireplace covers
- Mail slot covers
- Basement windows

Stitched Seams

If seams are stitched and magnets or steel tape is enclosed, place layers together as shown. Position magnet or steel on lining seam allowances. (Other seam allowances may be trimmed to reduce bulk.) Turn mat inside out and close opening by hand. If preferred, apply magnets or steel to outside edges after construction is completed.

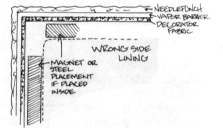

Bound Edges

If you choose to bind the edges of the mat and apply the magnets or steel tape to the outside, stack the layers together and hold edges with pins or basting. Bind edges with matching or contrasting bias strips. Tip: Use glue (Quik, Wilhold, FabTrim) to hold bias in place so it won't slip. Then stitch or glue to finish the edges.

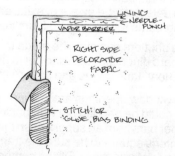

NOTE: The same basic effect can be achieved with Velcro used on outside edges for a tight seal. For small and odd shaped windows make a paper pattern first, then add seam allowances.

SHUTTERS

Shutters can be extremely efficient (when sealed and insulated) or terrific energy wasters. If you own louvered or fabric shutters, consider a shade behind them (or over them). One lady who had inside mounted shutters on the lower half of the window made an outside mount magnetic Roman Shade which pulls up out of the way, or drops down and seals right over the shutters. Looks great! Fabric filled and louvered shutters could have an insulating layer attached over the back, and weather stripping added. Solid shutters should be weather stripped.

SIMPLE POP-IN AND POP-ON SHUTTERS

The quickest way to create a shutter is to cut a piece of rigid foil-faced foam (from building supply) such as Thermax, High R Sheathing, or R-Max to fit the window opening. Make a paper or cardboard pattern to check snug fit. Then cut foam, tape edges for protection, and wrap with fabric (staple, glue, or fuse), or wallcovering. Add a lining piece on the back, a pull tab and voila! A friction-fit pop-in shutter.

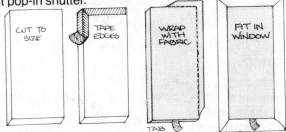

NOTE: Because foam insulating boards are flammable and can give off toxic gases, building codes require ceilings and walls to be covered with ½" *(1,3 cm)* of plasterboard or equivalent. Codes say nothing about window insulation—and there are arguments among experts about the toxicity of the smoke produced. Foam products do give off toxic gases when burned—but so do other household items: wood gives off carbon monoxide, wool gives off hydrogen cyanide. You should be aware of the potential fire hazard just as you should be aware of danger of fire from drapes, foam cushions, mattresses and other home furnishings. Install smoke detectors, be aware of exits, and keep aware of changes and developments related to rigid foam insulating products.

Simple shutters can even be made from several layers of corrugated cardboard glued together and cut to fit the window. Cover with foil to reflect heat, tape edges and cover with fabric. Friction fit into window.

If your window openings are in even inch increments or very close (so edges could be padded out with batting or needlepunch)—you may buy stretcher bars from art supply, push them together to form a frame. Use a carpenter's square to be sure the frame is square, then staple across the joints to reinforce them. Fill the center with batting, needlepunch, layers of cardboard, rigid foam, etc. or a combination of products. Wrap with fabric by centering the frame on the wrong side of fabric. Hold with push pins, then bring fabric over bars and staple at center top and bottom, keeping the fabric taut as shown. Repeat at sides so there is no slack in the fabric.

Start at the center of each strip and staple toward the corners, stopping about 1½" *(3,8 cm)* from the end. Do top and bottom first, then sides. To finish corners, smooth fabric along the stretcher bar, pull it snugly into a mitered fold and staple it in place. Pick up the remaining fabric and smooth it into a sharp corner, wrap it to the back and staple it on top of the first fold.

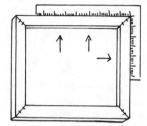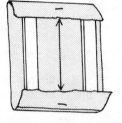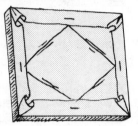

To finish corners, smooth fabric along the stretcher bar, pull it snugly into a mitered fold and staple it in place. Pick up the remaining fabric and smooth it into a sharp corner, wrap it to the back and staple it on top of the first fold.

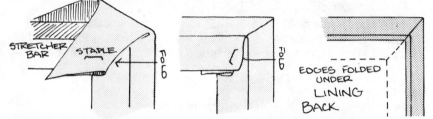

Finish the back of the shutter by stapling, gluing or fusing a piece of lining (fold raw edges under) in place. Add hinges if desired and weatherstripping if needed.

To make a pop-on shutter measure so shutter fits onto window frame or wall (when no frame is present.) Construct shutter by one of the methods just described. Place alternating magnet strips and peel and stick foam weatherstripping around back edge of shutter. On window frame place magnet strips (painted to match frame if desired) in same location so they will match when shutter is popped on and weather strip compresses to form seal. Or place steel tape on window frame—it will be less noticeable, especially if painted to match wall or frame.

To make a sturdier and thicker shutter two stretcher bar frames can be fastened together. This allows the use of 1½" foil-faced rigid foam (R-10) in the center, or use layers of batting and plastic vapor barrier stapled to one frame and then sandwiched between when frames are joined by stapling them together along the edges as shown. Wrap with fabric as outlined above. Simple, easy, efficient!

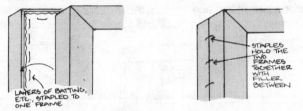

NOTE: If frame is padded with quilt batting and clear plastic vapor barrier, then wrapped with a relatively light colored fabric, a transluscent shutter can be created.

 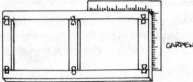

A simple wood frame built from 1" × 2" *(2,5 cm × 5 cm)* lumber can be filled with batting, foam, vapor barrier (on warm side), etc. Wrap as in above directions. Hinges may be added if desired and weatherstripping if needed.

Storage for friction-fit shutters may require some creativity, but it is not insurmountable:

- Hang them on the wall as wall art, stacked or singly
- Hide them under the bed or in a closet
- Slide them into a small wall niche built just for them
- Stash behind a folding screen, sofa, or wall storage unit
- Hang or stack behind a door

HINGED SHUTTERS

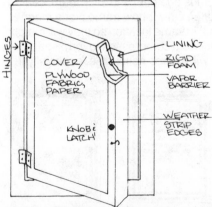

Hinged shutters may be solid or wood frame around layers of insulating material. The shutter can be single, or bi-fold type. There are many commercially made hinged shutters, shutter kits, plans, and articles on shutter making (see Suggested Reading). If this is the aproach you take, a little homework and research will be worthwhile. Costs can range from $.75/sq. ft. to $10.00/sq. ft., depending on type and materials. A general rule of thumb is that the investment should be recouped in fuel savings and tax credits in about five years.

CORNICES AND VALANCES

As the cost of energy rises, the use of cornices, valances and lambrequins will rise as well. These closed-top window toppers stop air currents from dropping in behind window treatments.

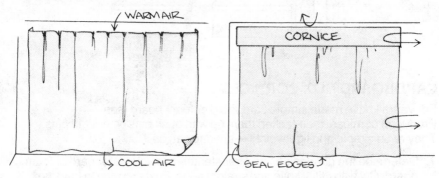

They don't have to look like a box—they can be flat, ruffled, swagged and pleated. And they DON'T have to weigh a ton or require a master carpenter.

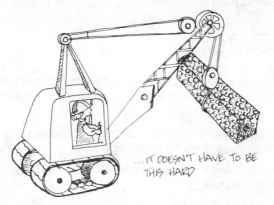

...IT DOESN'T HAVE TO BE THIS HARD

Cornices can also be used to conceal or unify layered window treatments. You might have a venetian blind and a roller shade or two all tucked up behind a simple cornice, each or all to be lowered as needed.

Anatomy of a Cornice:

TOP: Deep enough to clear treatment when drawn.

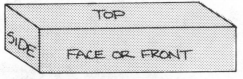

FACE: usually 1/6 to 1/9 of window height.

SIDE: Depends on treatment. Allow for drapery stackback.

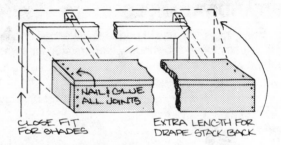

CLOSE FIT
FOR SHADES

EXTRA LENGTH FOR
DRAPE STACK BACK

NAIL & GLUE
ALL JOINTS

CARDBOARD BOX CORNICES

For years I have made simple cardboard or foam board (see Products) cornices, then tacked them up with push pins or straight pins. They're so simple and lightweight—anyone can do it.

1. Determine the dimensions and transfer them to your cardboard or foam board. Cut with utility knife and straight edge. Fold and tape to form 'box.'

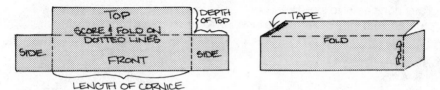

TOP — DEPTH OF TOP
SCORE & FOLD ON DOTTED LINES
SIDE — FRONT — SIDE
LENGTH OF CORNICE

TAPE — FOLD — FOLD

2. Staple or glue padding (Pellon Fleece, ThermolamPlus®, needlepunch, quilt batting) to cornice, wrapping it around the lower edges about 1" *(2,5 cm)*.

3. Center design of fabric on cornice and wrap loosely to determine placement. Cut fabric, allowing for wrapping room.

   (Mark fabric with water soluble transfer marker.) Wrap fabric and staple, glue, or fuse it in place.

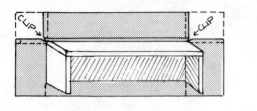

CLIP — CLIP

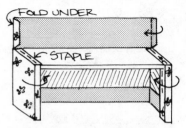

FOLD UNDER — STAPLE

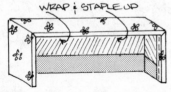

WRAP & STAPLE UP

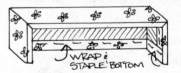

WRAP & STAPLE BOTTOM

4. To finish off the inside of the cornice, cut a strip of lining or off white fabric and staple, glue or fuse it on to conceal raw edges. (Fold raw edges of lining under ½" *(1,3 cm).*)

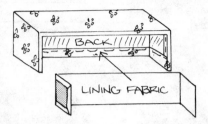

5. To mount the cornice at the window set it on the top of window frame and pound a couple push pins in to hold it; (or use straight pins or small nails.) To raise a cornice to a higher level, tack into the sides of the frame. If there is no frame—try tacking into the wall on an angle or mounting a curtain rod and set cornice on top. Small blocks of wood may also be tacked or glued to the wall and used for attaching the cornice.

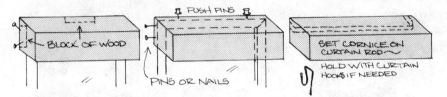

HINT: Consider flexible self-stick magnetic tape for mounting lightweight cornices.

MOUNTING BOARD

A board fastened above the window with angle irons, which are anchored to wall studs, creates a base on which many types of treatments are formed. You can even install shade brackets or other hardware on the underside of the board itself.

The board must be wide enough and long enough to clear the window treatment beneath—

CORNICE

1. Cut, score and fold a length of cardboard or foam board to fit front and sides of mounting board. Pad and cover with fabric. Tack it to outer edges of board, or leave fabric 'flange' to staple to the top of the board.

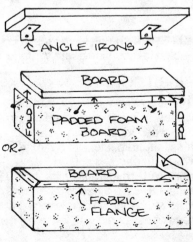

VALANCE

Make a pinch pleated valance to fit mounting board. Position a pleat on each corner. Hand whip a 2" *(5 cm)* fabric strip to the back of the valance near the top. Staple strip to board.

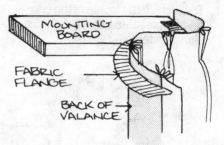

For a ruffled valance, seam and hem fabric to desired depth and double the finished width. Stitch on shirring tape. Pull up cords to gather fabric to fit mounting board. Tack on flange and staple to mounting board.

SWAGS AND CASCADES

Add flange to edge of swags and cascades, or just staple the top edge of the fabric to the mounting board.

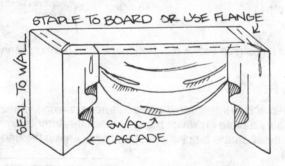

NOTE: Pre-shrunk snap tape or hook tape may be stitched to flange and stapled to mounting board to make removal of treatment for cleaning easier.

FLUSH CORNICE

This simple cornice fits within the window frame to coordinate with roller shade, venetian blind, cafe curtains, shutters, etc. Cut board to fit, wrap with padding and fabric. Attach to frame with angle irons. OR cut a piece of cardboard or foam board to fit opening. Pad and wrap with fabric. Tack to opening with straight pins or small fine nails. Color head of nail or pin with felt pen if it shows.

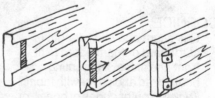

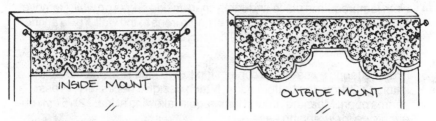

This cornice may also be made of wood painted or stained to match woodwork so it conceals the window treatment, but is very inconspicuous as part of the window.

NOTE: You will find more cornice construction and mounting ideas in DECORATING WITH FABRIC/An Idea Book. Cornice shapes and hem treatment ideas are found in THE SHADE BOOK, both by Judy Lindahl . . . ordering information on p. 128.

LAMBREQUINS

A lambrequin is essentially a cornice with long sides. They usually go clear to the floor, but may be shorter, depending on the design. It is a classic treatment that dates back centuries to royal European courts. In today's scheme of things it provides both top and side seals while adding a special decorative touch.

1. Measure from top of window molding + 1½" *(3,8 cm)* or desired height (approx. 10" *(25,5 cm)* above window) to floor. Measure width of window at sill (widest point) + 1½" *(3,8 cm)* or desired width to allow for drapery stack back if needed. These are inside measurements of lambrequin.

2. Use 1" × 4" *(2,5 cm × 10 cm)* or 1" × 6" *(2,5 × 15 cm)* pine for top and sides. Nail and glue together.

3. For the face use 1" × 10" *(2,5 × 25,5 cm)* or plywood strips cut to size or use upsom board (see Products) cut to size from 6" *(15 cm)* to 12" *(30,5 cm)*. Use mending plates to join face pieces if necessary. Nail and glue face to sides and top.

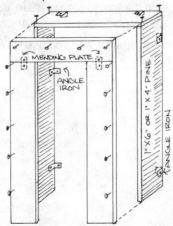

4. Hold lambrequin in place and lightly mark inside edges on wall. Remove lambrequin and fasten 1½" *(3,8 cm)* angle irons to the wall. Try to anchor to wall studs at top with 1¼" *(3,2 cm)* screws and use hollow-wall anchors for sides.

5. Prepare fabric by sewing a center strip to two long side pieces. Stop stitching 2" from the bottom edge. Match design if necessary. Press seams open. Measure around lambrequin, allowing at least 2" *(5 cm)* on each side for wrapping ease.

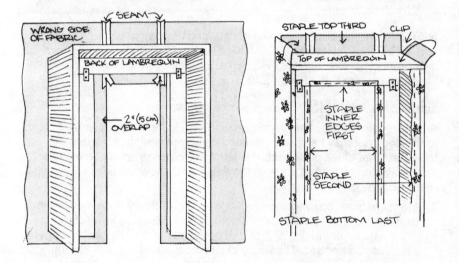

6. Pad the lambrequin with layer(s) of batting or needlepunch (Pellon fleece, ThermoLam Plus). Staple or glue in place, butting edges to splice.

7. Place fabric on top of the padding. Center and smooth in place. Pull fabric around inner edges of the lambrequin and staple. Then start on the outer edges, next staple the top, folding sides in first. Finally pull bottom edge taut, folding excess in, and staple bottom.

8. Hold lambrequin in place against wall and use ⅝" *(1,5 cm)* screws to attach it to the angle irons.

UPHOLSTERED/ FABRIC WALLS

Upholstered walls had their earliest beginnings centuries ago when heavy tapestries and fabric hangings were used for covering interior walls. In addition to color and design they gave insulation and acoustical benefits to large drafty rooms. For the most part wall coverings were developed to imitate fabric. Now, fabric is gaining favor again as a beautiful and practical wall covering.

Upholstered or padded, fabric-covered walls have long been a favorite of interior designers. They create a soft and opulent look in moires, silks, and velvets and soft, cozy looks in prints of all types. The added touch of quilting or tufting contributes to the mood.

Upholstered walls may cost more due to the extra layer of padding beneath. However, they can hide badly damaged, textured or unattractive walls. In many cases no preparation, patching or stripping, will be necessary before the walls can be covered. Thus the final cost may be no different from other methods requiring more initial preparation, especially costly labor. As mentioned, upholstered walls give the added benefit of insulating and sound dampening (especially nice in childrens' rooms) and they magically cut outside noise interference from neighbors or busy streets. Even one upholstered wall in a room can cut the noise level noticeably. Later, both the fabric and padding may be retrieved and re-used if desired when the treatment is removed, even years from now.

Now is the time to consider whether or not you want to add a vapor barrier to the walls before they are covered. (See p. 121.) In addition to vapor barrier paint you may consider a layer of plastic or even aluminum foil (which reflects radiant heat back into the room) beneath the fabric.

I don't know of any work that has been undertaken to study the R-value of an upholstered wall. There are many variables that make this difficult—among them the type of materials each person chooses, and more specifically, how they are applied.

You may not be upholstering all or even most of the walls in your home—but if you have considered it, it is nice to know you can enjoy energy benefits from your efforts plus gain a spectacular wall treatment in the process. If energy savings is your prime motivator you will want to consider the outside walls for padding. If a cozy feeling is your goal, any wall may be chosen. In a bedroom you might select the wall behind the bed, which then becomes a focal point.

The padding will be more apparent if you select a solid or muted design for your fabric. On the other hand, the small errors that may occur for the do-it-yourselfer are MUCH LESS NOTICEABLE on busier prints.

PADDING

Several types of padding may be used. Polyester quilt batting ½" (1,3 cm) or 1" (2,5 cm) thick, which is available by the yard or in larger comforter size pieces, will give a soft, puffy look. The thicker the padding, the puffier the wall. Look for resin treated or glazed batting which will hold its shape and need less support against sagging.

Foam sheeting ¼" (6 mm) is quite easy to work with since it tends to cling to the wall and the fabric clings to it. You may also use polyester fleece (Pellon fleece, Thermolam® Plus, needlepunch, etc.), though it is flatter and will add less dimension to the finished wall.

STAPLE GUNS

Since you will be doing a lot of stapling with this technique, you may wish to consider purchasing an electric staple gun which has the power to shoot six staple lengths with equal ease. Watch for guns on sale in home improvement centers and hardware stores. Keep in mind that most of the electric models do not fit up tight into corners because the motor extends in front of the stapling head. In this case you may need a hand stapler for tight areas, or you will have to plan to use a wider band of trim or molding to conceal the space.

If you are forced to put some staples in vertically on a horizontal line, you will need staples twice as close together to achieve the same holding power.

BEFORE YOU BEGIN

Look at the Room to help you decide where you want upholstered walls. The fewer objects you have to go around, the simpler it will be. Where do you want the focal point? Where do you most need insulation or sound dampening?

Measure Walls for height and to determine whether ceiling is straight. Measure floor to ceiling in 3 or 4 places

What is the Construction of the Wall? Plaster, tile, concrete block, sheetrock or paneling are possible. Test your staple gun to see if you will be able to staple directly to the wall. If not, you may need to apply furring strips to the wall first. Furring strips are thin wood strips which can be purchased at lumber yards, or you can saw a board into thin ⅜" *(1 cm)* or ¼" *(6mm)* strips on a table saw. The strips are used as a 'buffer' so fabric can be stapled to hard or uneven surfaces. They can be nailed or attached with an adhesive (such as paneling adhesive applied with a caulking gun).

If needed, apply furring strips along ceiling, floor, each side of a corner and vertically where seams will lie. Outline doors, windows, and other openings.

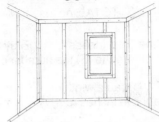

Another alternative is to have FabriTrak® wall system custom applied in part or total. (See p. 93.)

NOTE: If furring strips or FabriTrak® are used, surface wiring will be covered by the fabric. Thus you may find it convenient to relocate or add outlets or switches that may have posed problems for you.

Selecting Fabric is a Critical Step. For best results choose a non-stretchy fabric of medium weight. Padding is most obvious with solids such as velvet (run the nap up for richness, down for sheen and resistance to catching dust), and moire which gives a wonderfully subtle texture to a room. Allover prints are easiest to apply, show fewer errors in application, make a room feel cozy, but require care in matching design at seams. It is best to avoid stripes and plaids. Even the experts have trouble keeping the lines straight and even. Diagonal prints, i.e. lattice designs, bandana prints, etc., make a room visually exciting and are worth considering.

If Possible, read the chapter on Fabric Walls in DECORATING WITH FABRIC/An Idea Book by Judy Lindahl. It will answer most any questions you may have about the selection and handling of fabric for wall application.

MEASURING

Calculate the number of fabric strips or panels that you will need to cover the area you have chosen.

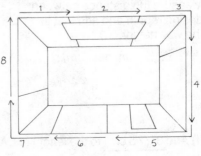

STEP 1—DETERMINE THE NUMBER OF PANELS

1. Add the corner to corner measurements of the walls to be covered.

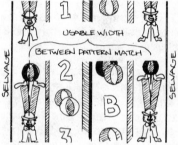

(A) _____ inches *(cm)*
(B) _____ inches *(cm)*
(C) _____ inches *(cm)*
(D) _____ inches *(cm)*
_____
(E) _____ TOTAL inches *(cm)*

2. Divide the Total inches *(cm)* (E) by the usable width of fabric in inches *(cm)* to determine (F) the number of panels needed.

$$\text{Usable width of fabric in inches } (cm) \overline{)\,\underset{\text{(E) Total inches } (cm)}{\text{(F) _____ No. of panels needed*}}}$$

*Add an extra panel if the number is uneven.
Example: 6 panels + 24" *(61 cm)* = 7 panels

NOTE: Measure actual usable inches *(cm)* of the design. This eliminates selvages and overlap.

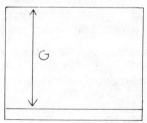

STEP 2—DETERMINE PANEL LENGTH

1. Measure ceiling to baseboard

(G) _____ inches *(cm)*

2. Measure the distance between design repeat and add that to the wall height.

(H) _____ inches *(cm)*

3. (I) Add 3" *(7,5 cm)* to the length of EACH PANEL for handling ease.

NOTE: I usually do not subtract for doors and windows unless there are many and they are large and occupy space nearly floor to ceiling. You will always have some extra fabric pieces, but they are great for pillows, etc.

4. Total the above measurements:
   (G) _____ inches *(cm)*
   (H) _____ inches *(cm)*
   (I)   3   inches *(7,5 cm)*
   _____
   (J) _____ Panel Length in inches *(cm)*

STEP 3—CONVERT PANEL LENGTHS TO YARDS (Meters)

1. $(J) \times (F)$ = Total inches *(cm)* needed (K)

   Multiply panel length (J) times number of panels (F), to determine total fabric needed (K).

2. $36'' \ (91,5 \ cm) \overline{)\dfrac{(L) \ No. \ of \ Yds. \ (m)}{(K) \ Total \ inches \ (cm)}}$

   Divide total length (K) by 36" *(91,5 cm)* to determine yards *(m)* of fabric needed.

NOTE: It is a good idea to add a yard or two for leeway, and more if you are planning to make curtains, shades, etc.

For Padding
Use same basic directions, however seams and edges will be butted together, so no extra allowance is needed for handling ease.
(Eliminate item 3 in step 2 above.)

COVERING THE WALL

1. Staple batting to all wall areas to be covered. Staple along edges approximately every 12" *(30,5 cm)*. On large wall areas you may need a few staples in the middle to add support if the padding tends to sag. If you use two layers for depth, staple the first layer horizontally and the second vertically.

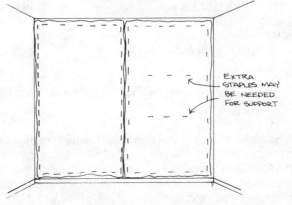

EXTRA STAPLES MAY BE NEEDED FOR SUPPORT

HINT: If you will be covering an outside corner, staple an 8" *(20,5 cm)* strip of batting over the corner first, then add the other layer or layers of batting in the normal way. This gives an extra cushion to the corner and reduces abrasion to the fabric.

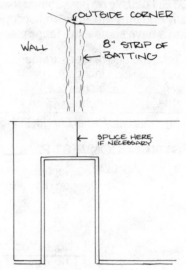

2. Cut fabric panels the desired length plus handling ease. (Be sure to match design if needed.) Seam individual panels together to create a wall-size panel or larger. If you cannot handle a room-size panel, try to splice in the short areas, such as over a door.

ENERGY TIP If possible, invite (cajole, bribe, etc.) a friend to help during the hanging process. It can be done alone—nearly any decorating project can—but it is so much easier with help. (It's YOUR energy that is saved this time.)

3. Make a short clip or mark at top and bottom of starting location on the fabric panel. (Usually the center of a panel that will be centered on the wall.) Mark a plumb line at this starting point on the wall. This will be keyed to the clips in your fabric. If you are not using furring strips at seam locations, additional plumb lines may be needed to assure fabric is kept straight.

To make a plumb line, attach a string to a plumb bob or heavy object such as a pair of scissors. Rub the cord with colored chalk and attach it to the top of the wall. Hold the weight at the baseboard and snap the line against the wall. The vertical mark is your guide.

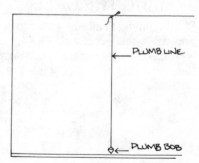

NOTE: You do not HAVE to chalk the string, but it is very helpful.

4. Start at the center of a wall, fold under the handling ease and staple or use push pins—the long point kind, ⅝" *(1,5 cm)* from stationery stores work best. Continue toward the corners keeping fabric taut and smooth. Staple the top edge first. Work from center and alternately toward corners. Staple sides next and bottom last.

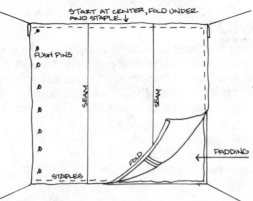

Here's a neat trick for getting smooth, strong inside corners: wrap a length of quarter round or cove molding with fabric, either cut to match your design or on the bias for contrast. Glue fabric in place around molding, then fasten molding into the corner with 4 or 5 finishing nails.

If you are ENDING on an outside corner, use a furring strip or piece of window molding, wrap fabric around it and secure with finishing nails. If you are framing the walls with furring strips, leave the one along the outside corner loose enough that you can tuck the fabric in before nailing it flat.

INSIDE CORNERS   OUTSIDE CORNERS

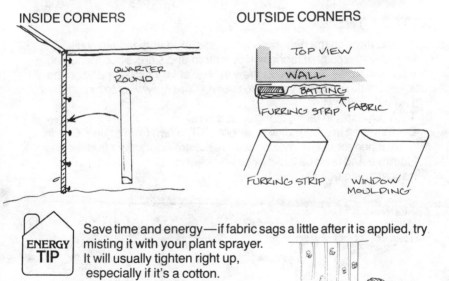

Save time and energy—if fabric sags a little after it is applied, try misting it with your plant sprayer. It will usually tighten right up, especially if it's a cotton.

ENERGY TIP

TUFTED WALLS

This variation of upholstered walls is made possible by using upholsterer's tacks, even thumbtacks to create a tufted look on the wall. If you have applied fabric over dry wall (sheet rock) construction, you should be able to pound tacks directly into the wall. If walls will not take the tacks, a thin layer, ⅜" (1 cm) of plywood may be applied to the wall first as a base for the tacks.

NOTE: If you want the tack color to closely match fabric color, pound tacks lightly into a board and spray paint them. Then pad the hammer to keep paint from chipping.

ANOTHER QUICK TRICK FOR CREATING A TUFTED LOOK:
Cut 6" (15 cm) lengths of yarn. Fold the yarns back and forth as illustrated. Staple over them at the place where you wish the tufting to occur. Fluff up the yarns to hide the staple. Voila!! Tufted wall.

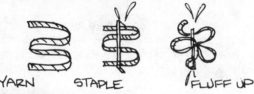

YARN   STAPLE   FLUFF UP

TO TUFT THE WALL:

First, read through the directions for upholstered and padded walls. Allow greater excess of fabric at top, bottom and sides since the tufting process will cause the fabric to draw in. The amount will depend on the thickness of the padding you have chosen. You may want to experiment with an old sheet.
1. Tack or push-pin fabric along ceiling line.
2. Begin tufting in center of wall, about 30" (76 cm) from ceiling. Continue across horizontally—making sure tacks are equidistant from ceiling. Remove and replace tacks or pins at ceiling as necessary to adjust fabric.

SAME DISTANCE FROM CEILING

TACK THIS ROW FIRST

TACK 2nd

TACK 3rd

TACK 4th

ETC.

HINT: A geometric pattern makes tufting easier since you can follow the pattern in the fabric rather than measuring for placement of the tacks or staples.

3. Drive tacks in rows above, and then below, first row, checking often to be sure rows are straight. Turn fabric under at sides, top, bottom and openings. Tack or staple.
4. Edges may be covered with molding, braid, gimp or welting if desired.

NOTE: If your padding is not too thick, you can successfully tuft a wall by following directions for upholstered walls first, then apply tacks as the finishing touch.

QUILT COVERED WALLS

Quilts are often hung on walls to soften the look and mood of a room. Generally, they are not installed wall to wall. However it is quite possible to use pieced and quilted fabric for larger installations. You may create your own or purchase quilted fabric by the yard. Fabrics that are quilted with a thin foam layer (placemat fabrics) are stable and very easy to install. Because of the bulk, the edges are usually butted together. If they need to be concealed, braid, gimp, ribbon or wood molding can be applied. Quilt covered walls give a homey, cozy look and can be appropriate for any room in the house.

FABRI TRAK®

Fabri Trak® Wall Covering System consists of specially designed fireproof vinyl channels developed a few years ago as a speedy, attractive, efficient way to apply fabric to walls. Once installed, the track can be re-used over and over with new and different fabrics. It can be applied without advance preparation of the wall surface, and can go on sheet rock, plaster, concrete block, tile or wood surfaces, claims the manufacturer.

Originally the system was made available to the do-it-yourselfer. Track came in 4' *(122 cm)* lengths which retailed at about $2.50 each. They could then be cut and mounted with "screws, nails, or silicone live rubber cement or other appropriate bonding agent." The manufacturer has since come to feel that because of the details of installing track around the room, fixtures, outlets, etc., it is best custom-installed. This may be the do-it-yourselfer's loss. However, you might consider having the track custom installed, but then install the fabric yourself. Because the system gives a smooth finished edge, there is no need for gimp, welting or trim unless you specifically desire it. Thus the cost of track installed may be offset by reduced preparation, no need for trim, and time savings. It may be well worth comparing, and considering. For more information, consult your local interior designer or contact Fabri Trak® directly (see Resources).

SHIRRED WALLS

A wonderful effect can be achieved with shirred (gathered) walls. They also add to the insulation and acoustical factor because of the dead air spaces created in the folds of the fabric. Though shirring takes a lot of fabric, it is fairly simple to do since the panels need not be sewn together. Edges can be hidden in the folds. This leaves yards of fabric literally "undamaged" which makes them retrievable and re-usable at a later date. Sheets are a natural for this method. They are lightweight enough to gather nicely, and wide enough to make them an economical choice. Detailed directions for measuring and installation can be found in Judy Lindahl's DECORATING WITH FABRIC/An Idea Book.

Photo Courtesy of Van Luit & Co., Photography: George R. Szanik

SHIRRED FABRIC insulates walls and adds accent to the bed. Warm colors and soft lines help capture the mood.

FABRIC WALLS (Direct Application)

Fabric covered walls create a special mood and feeling in a room and are one easy way to make a room really spectacular. While upholstered walls give the most depth, fabric applied directly is less expensive and less time consuming as well, and it can still conceal texture, color or damaged walls.

The mood of the room can be controlled by the type of fabric you choose—formal, informal, elegant, cozy, etc. If you choose to staple fabric to walls the technique is basically the same as for upholstered walls, but with no padding. The only real difference is that panels can be handled individually rather than being seamed. You may also wish to consider other methods of application such as using liquid starch (one of my favorite methods), wallpaper paste, glue, double-faced tape.

Because I have covered tips and techniques for all of these methods in my book DECORATING WITH FABRIC/An Idea Book, I am not including detailed instructions here. Space limitations make it impossible to do the job as completely as I feel needs to be done for the do-it-yourselfer. (See p. 128 for ordering information.)

Photo Courtesy of Pennsylvania House

FABRIC ON WALLS and padded lambrequins add to the effect and efficiency of this well designed room.

DOUBLE WELTING

Double welting is the added touch that makes a fabric covered wall truly spectacular. It is glued or tacked around walls to conceal staples or raw fabric edges. Traditionally, welting or cording is made on the bias so it shapes around curves and corners. It takes a bit more time and fabric, but is worth it if the fabric demands.

Because walls have long straight expanses, it will be cheaper and easier to make welting on the straight of grain if your fabric is light to medium weight. Heavy upholstery types will still require bias construction. You may have your welting made by an upholsterer or you may decide to make it yourself. Here is a simple method.

1. Cut strips of bias 3″ *(7,5 cm)* wide. See below for how to make continuous bias since you will be needing very long pieces.

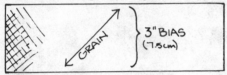

2. Position welting cord on the inside of the fabric strip. Bring raw edges together.

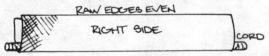

3. Lay second welting cord on top, next to first cord.

4. Fold fabric back over middle of the cords, using a wide zig-zag presser foot, and a longer stitch—5 to 6 stitches per inch *(2,5 cm)*. Keep folding and stitching until the welt is finished. (Your stitches should be slightly loose.) Trim any excess fabric near the stitching line.

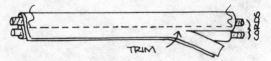

NOTE: Some upholstery suppliers carry pre-joined double cording. Just wrap fabric around the cords and stitch down the middle.

5. Run a dull knife or spoon edge between the cords to push the stitching into the welts. Pinch welts together to help shape and tighten them.

6. Glue welting in place around ceiling, floor, corners if necessary, and around doors and windows. Use a fast tack white craft glue such as

Wilhold, Fabri Trim, Quik, Velverette. If you're handy with a hot glue gun, you might try that. Practice on a scrap first.

7. Curve the welting at corners. If pieces must be spliced, clip cording back about ½" *(1,3 cm)* from ends of fabric, fold one end under, overlap the other.

HOW TO MAKE CONTINUOUS BIAS

1. Fold a length of fabric on true bias as shown. Cut off the triangle formed.
2. Draw bias lines for as much cording as you will need. Cut off the excess fabric.

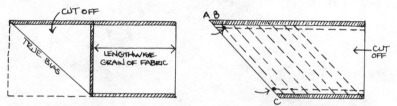

3. Form a sleeve, right sides together, and pin the selvages together. Be sure to pin corner C to point B. Stitch with ½" *(1,3 cm)* seam allowance. Press the seam and then cut along the lines starting at B/C and continuing in a spiral to the end of the sleeve.

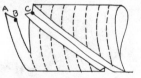

JOINING THE BIAS

The bias is joined by placing two strips with the right sides together at right angles. Stitch a ½" *(1,3 cm)* seam allowance. Press open and trim off the corners if desired.

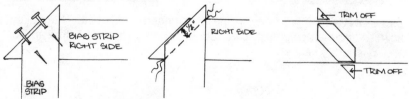

ESTIMATING YARDAGE (amounts are approximate)

½ yd *(46 cm)* of 36" *(90 cm)* fabric yields 5 yds *(4,60 m)*
½ yd *(46 cm)* of 48" *(122 cm)* fabric yields 8 yds *(7,35 m)*
½ yd *(46 cm)* of 54" *(140 cm)* fabric yields 10 yds *(9,15 m)*

Photo Courtesy of Stacy Fabrics Corp., A Subsidiary of Shire Nat'l. Corp.

QUILTS ON WALLS, wainscoting and table runners padded with Thermolam Plus (needlepunch), plump pillows, fabric accents on the light fixture add to this cozy country kitchen.

BEDS and BEDROOMS

While most aspects of energy saving decorating apply to any room in the house, there are some that are most common to bedrooms—and specifically the bed. Nighttime comfort can be controlled and increased in a number of ways.

Unfortunately, the habit for many in the past has been to turn the thermostat up until the desired level of warmth was attained. With soaring fuel costs this becomes an expendable solution. Most psychological tricks aren't going to be of much benefit at night when the room is pitch black, so you'll need to plan warmth or cooling into your decorating scheme.

"I PAINTED THIS ROOM SUNSHINE YELLOW... BUT I DON'T FEEL WARM NOW!"

This may require just a minor juggling of the look of the bed, where it is placed, or the way it is dressed—or you may do a whole 'make-over' in conjuction with a redecorating project.

New trends in bed-dressing favor softer, plumper, quilted looks—which can easily be incorporated into a cozy room decor. The comforter thus takes the place of bedspread and even blankets. Fortunately, these 'un-made' or open bed looks can adapt equally to spare, uncluttered decorating themes. The end result is simply that you have controlled and created the warmth or coolness you prefer for your bed.

Your favorite style of decor need not be tossed out because it doesn't fit the plump or open look. There are many solutions and approaches to consider in achieving the degree of nighttime comfort you desire. Your solution may actually be a combination of several. Here are some to consider:

LAYER IT ON . . .

More and more people are turning to texture and layers. Several light layers of clothing keep us warmer than a single heavy layer, because of the insulating dead air spaces created between the layers. The same principle applies to bedding, and layers can be removed or added as seasons demand, allowing you to retain your favorite bedspread.

Upholstered Headboard

Uncovered Pillows

Pillow Shams

Flannel or Decorator Sheets

Comforter

Dust Ruffle

QUILTS

These pieced and stitched beauties can add warmth and texture to the bed and room, too. Heirloom or soon-to-be, their decorating value is obvi-ous. Many people use them as wall-hangings, table covers, chair throws, etc. The tradi-tional quilt was thinner with a single layer of batting. Many of today's contemporary quilts are thicker and loftier due to improvements in fiberfil batts.

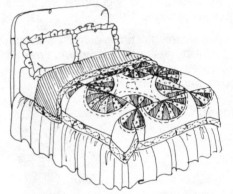

COMFORTERS

Light, lofty feather down and poly fiberfil comforters are increasingly popular. Though the price of down keeps rising, do-it-yourself kits (Altra, with easy sewing technique, Frost-line, Sundown, etc.) help re-duce costs. Fiberfill can give as much as 80% of the warmth of down for the weight, yet costs are considerably lower.

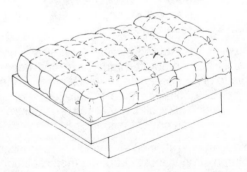

A comforter is usually shorter and narrower than a bedspread. This makes the platform bed a good choice. If you prefer a more traditional bed you may want a coordinated or contrasting dust ruffle to give the bed a finished, well-dressed look. (See dust ruffle ideas and directions.)

ENERGY TIP

If your comforter doesn't come in fabric to match your decor or if you redecorate, consider making a simple slip-cover (see Duvets). An added benefit—the comforter will need cleaning much less often, and the original cover will last longer.

How To Make a Simple Comforter

Determining Yardage: Comforters usually end about 3"-4" *(7,5-10 cm)* below the mattress on the sides (B). Length is determined by whether you want the comforter to tuck under the pillows or be folded down in open bed (A), or whether you want additional length for tuck-in so the comforter can be pulled up and over the pillows (C).

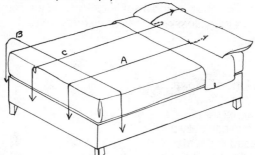

If the comforter must be pieced or seamed, a full width panel is placed in the center with side panels as needed. Avoid a center seam.

NOTE: Machine quilting, hand quilting or tying of yarns, which keeps the batting in place, also causes the sides of the comforter to 'pull in,' thus reducing over-all finished size, so allow a little extra length and width. The thicker the comforter, the more this occurs. All-over quilting causes more 'take-up' than yarn tying.

CONSTRUCTION:

1. Cut and seam top and bottom pieces to create necessary width. Round the corners if desired.

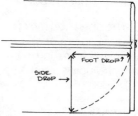

2. Lay top and bottom pieces right sides together, anchor with a few pins.
3. Lay the layer or layers of quilt batting (available in twin, full, queen, king sizes or by the yard) which have been pieced if necessary, on the wrong side of the top comforter piece. Pin in place along all the edges and intermittently in the middle as needed.
4. Stitch around the comforter leaving an opening for turning at center top. Trim and clip corners to reduce bulk and trim the batting close to the stitching line.

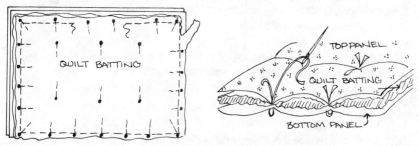

5. Turn the comforter right side out, close the opening by hand or machine. Lay comforter out and mark it with pins or chalk at about 10"-12" *(25,5-30,5 cm)* intervals. Thread a large needle with two strands of washable yarn. Push the needle down through all layers then right back up through all layers. Knot the yarn ends securely with square knots. Clip yarns to about ¾" *(2cm)*.

NOTE: For a change of pace and a soft look try tying the comforter with perle cotton embroidery floss or nylon upholstery thread. The ties will be less noticeable.

DUVETS

One variation of the comforter called the duvet (doo-vay) creates a very simple bed covering style. It is basically a comforter encased in sheets to match your pillows and bottom sheet, similar to a comforter cover.

However, the duvet is meant to be the ONLY top layer, with no top sheet underneath between it and the bottom sheet. This European import is great for the spare look and for children's rooms. Bed-making is a snap! Just fluff the pillow, smooth the bottom sheet and fluff up the duvet.

NOTE: The open bed look features visible pillows which can be propped slightly, or if you prefer shams—consider a separate set of inexpensive pillows which can be left in the shams all the time, saving the wear and tear and time of slipping them on and off daily. (See directions for making pillow shams.)

Duvet Covers
A duvet cover may be nothing more than a 'large pillowcase' with some type of fastener. It is usually made from a set of sheets that matches or coordinates with bottom sheet and pillows.

Envelope Cover:
1. Measure comforter length plus 4" *(10cm)* and width plus 2" *(5cm)*. Cut and seam fabric or sheets to these dimensions.
2. Place fabric right sides together. Stitch sides and bottom with a ½" *(1,3 cm)* seam. Trim corners, turn right side out and press.
3. Turn top edge down 1" *(2,5 cm)* then 1" *(2,5 cm)* again to form a double 1" *(2,5 cm)* hem. Press and stitch.
4. Make buttonholes every 8"-10" *(20,5-25,5 cm)* along one side of the top edge. Sew buttons on the inside of the opposite side, or use 1" *(2,5 cm)* lengths of nylon fastener tape or snap tape by the yard.

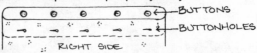

5. Slip comforter inside the cover and button it up. Your duvet is ready.

FLIP TOP COVER

1. Measure width plus 2" *(5cm)* and length plus 4" *(10 cm)* for bottom piece. Measure width plus 2" *(5 cm)* and length plus 16" *(40,5 cm)* for top piece.
2. Turn, press and stitch a double 1" *(2,5 cm)* hem on top edge of each piece.
3. Fold 12" *(30,5 cm)* toward right side on top piece, then pin top and bottom sections right sides together.

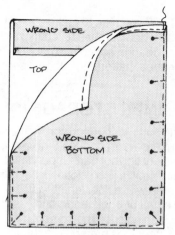

4. Stitch sides and bottom edges with a ½" *(1,3 cm)* seam allowance, backtacking for reinforcement at top edges.
5. Trim corners, turn right side out and press. Slip comforter into cover, then flip the 12" *(30,5 cm)* flap over the top of the cover, thus enclosing the comforter inside.

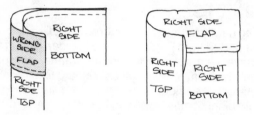

SUMMER REPLACEMENT—A SHEET COVER

In hot summer climates the comforter or quilt may not be needed. To maintain the look of your bed and keep you cool—make a decorative sheet cover. Just cut a sheet down to the size of the comforter and bind off and trim the edges with eyelet, ribbon or the scraps from your sheet.

ENERGY TIP

If you need more warmth, a light weight blanket or cotton flannel sheet may replace the comforter, topped by the sheet cover. Or try a cotton flannel sheet or flannel yardage seamed to size (PRE-SHRUNK) cut the same size as your pre-shrunk sheet cover. Sew the two with right sides together, leaving an opening for turning it right side out. Add trim in the seam or apply afterward if desired.

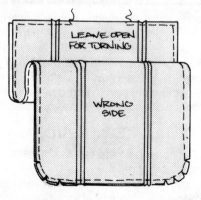

NOTE: If you plan to make a sheet cover for your bed, you will need to plan ahead when purchasing comforters and sheets. Because decorator sheet styles change so rapidly (every 6 months for some designs), you may find your sheet pattern has been discontinued if you try to purchase at a later date.

SUMMER STORAGE IDEAS

In the summer comforters, quilts, duvets may need to be stored if your climate is warm enough that they are not needed. This may require a little creativity on your part, depending on the amount and type of storage space available. If a linen closet is not available, consider under a round table covered with a floor length cloth, in a chest or trunk, under the bed, behind a folding screen. One ingenious method is to use it as a wall hanging behind the bed, or elsewhere in the room, or sew a large floor pillow duvet and use it as an accent pillow.

FLANNEL SHEETS

After years of being nearly forgotten, you can now readily find cotton flannel sheets. Usually imported from England where the idea of thermal under-wear for the bed never went out of style, they are warmer and softer to climb into on a cold night. You may want to save your hard finish cool cotton or cotton/poly sheets for hotter months. In cool weather the flannel sheets plus sheet cover or light blanket may be all you'll need.

Common sources are mail order catalogs, if you can't find them locally in stores. Look for sheets that have been pre-shrunk or have a full shrinkage allowance built in, especially if they are 100% cotton. Some styles have polyester reinforcement at corners for fitted styles; others are a blend of cotton/polyester for softness and strength. The higher the cotton content, the SOFTER and MORE ABSORBENT, too.

ELECTRIC BLANKETS

The electricity used to run an electric blanket is less than would be needed to keep the furnace up all night to keep the same degree of warmth. In addition the electric blanket enables one to create a trimmer, more tailored look for the bed if the plump and lofty style is not for you. Dual controls allow comfort for bed partners with different 'body thermostats.' Coordinating the electric blanket with some of the other techniques, i.e. flannel sheets, or 'space sheets' may allow you to set the blanket on an even lower setting.

UNDER COVER AIDS

Capitalizing on the fact that heat rises, there are several products on the market that put the warmth under you instead of on top. Electric bed pads warm gently from below with varying amounts of heat—none at shoulders, moderate amounts at waist level and most at the feet.

The space age created a need for super lightweight, strong, heat reflecting materials. These new products have begun to find their way into energy conserving products. For example there is a family of 'bed warmers' or 'space sheets' which are placed under the regular sheet. They are made with a reflective layer that stops heat from passing through and radiates it back toward the body. They are available in twin to king sizes and generally retail from about $7 to $12, or make your own from Astrolar.

DUST RUFFLES

Dust ruffles may be gathered, pleated, or boxed (pleats at corners). They hide the box spring and combine well with comforters and duvets. They are also used often with quilts and short coverlet bedspreads. Lightweight fabrics gather well, medium and heavy fabrics will be most attractive in smooth, pleated types.

Ruffles and side strips can be attached to a flat piece of fabric cut to fit the top of the box spring, to a fitted sheet slipped over the box spring, or directly to the edge of the box spring.

DETERMINING YARDAGE:

1. Depth: Measure top edge of box spring to floor (A). Add 4" *(10 cm)* for hem, seam allowance, and turn back.
2. Length: Measure distance around the two sides and foot (B). Add 1" *(2,5 cm)* for each seam needed to combine strips to achieve measurement B.

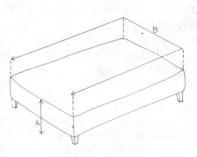

DOUBLE FULLNESS (B × 2) allows for a gathered ruffle OR a box pleated ruffle with 2½" *(6,5 cm)* deep pleats 10" *(25,5 cm)* apart.

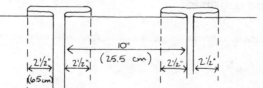

TRIPLE FULLNESS (B × 3) yields a full gathered ruffle OR a box pleated ruffle with 2½" *(6,5 cm)* deep pleats 5" *(12,5 cm)* apart.

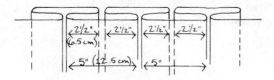

B PLUS 40"(101,5 cm) yields a
tailored dust ruffle with 5" (12,5
cm) deep box pleats at
corners of foot of the bed.

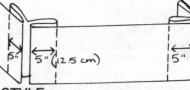

CONSTRUCTION OF RUFFLED STYLE:

1. Place a fitted sheet on box spring, or if you prefer, cut a piece of fabric or
   sheet the same size as the top of the box spring and use this as the
   dust ruffle base. Mark top edge of sheet or fabric every 12" (30,5 cm) on
   sides and bottom.

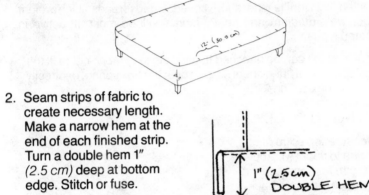

2. Seam strips of fabric to
   create necessary length.
   Make a narrow hem at the
   end of each finished strip.
   Turn a double hem 1"
   (2.5 cm) deep at bottom
   edge. Stitch or fuse.

3. Make short clips every 12" (30,5 cm) along top edge of strip.
4. Use one of the following methods to gather the ruffle strip.
   A. Make two rows of basting stitches along top edge—one row ¾" (2
      cm) from the edge, one row 1" (2,5 cm) from the edge. Use bobbin
      twist on the bobbin for strength. Draw up evenly into gathers.
   B. Stitch double cord shirring tape 1" (2,5 cm) from top edge. Knot cords
      so they won't pull out as you draw up the gathers.
   C. Zig-zag over strong fine cord placed 1" (2,5 cm) from top edge of
      fabric. Draw up gathers.

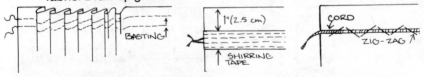

5. Adjust gathers to fit marks on edge
   of sheet. Pin ruffle to sheet, right
   sides together, side hems at head of
   bed, edge of ruffle even with edge of
   box spring. Remove sheet and ruffle
   and stitch ruffle in place 1" (2,5 cm)
   from raw edge.

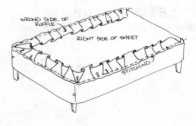

6. Flip ruffle over into position. Stitch again next to seam to hold gathers in place.

CONSTRUCTION OF PLEATED STYLES:

Pin strip to base fabric right sides together, starting with a pleat at center bottom, pin pleats in place, working around to the head of the bed. Make any small adjustments needed to allow pleats to fall at corners of foot.

For tailored box style place a box pleat 5" *(12,5 cm)* deep at each corner of foot of bed.

PILLOW SHAMS

Pillow shams are often combined with quilts and comforters for the open-bed look. Shams are loose fitting covers, which often have a ruffled, pleated, or eyelet border. A lapped opening across the back allows the pillow to be slipped in and out easily.

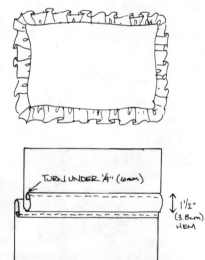

1. Cut front section in one piece according to the size of your pillow. Cut back sections in two pieces allowing 4" *(3,8 cm)* hem on each piece to form overlay. Make a 1½" *(3,8 cm)* hem on each piece, then overlap and pin sections so they fit the front section.

2. Pin ruffle to right side of top pillow section adjusting fullness at corners. Lay bottom section in place. Pin. Stitch with ½" *(1,3 cm)* seam allowance. Trim corners, turn sham right side out through overlap. Press.

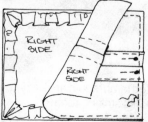

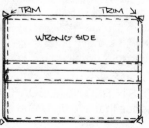

THE ENCLOSED BED

Another concept being re-discovered is the built-in or enclosed bed, which then reduces the area that needs to be heated or cooled. In winter you can take advantage of the 360+ b.t.u.s per hour each adult gives off at night.

There are a variety of approaches to achieving this concept, and of course you need either to build your decorating concept around it, or seek a method that blends in.

One simple solution utilizes floor to ceiling draperies which slide on ceiling mounted tracks. If your ceiling cannot take the tracks directly, consider mounting boards in a U-shape over the bed and attaching the track to the boards. A second strip of wood or decorative molding can be added to the edge of the wood piece to conceal the hardware and provide a finished, enclosed cornice look. The frame can be stained or painted. Fabric can be stapled tautly across the inside of the frame to provide an inside canopy, if desired.

UPHOLSTERED HEADBOARDS

Headboards, padded or upholstered to match the bedding, are a current favorite. Basically they are made of plywood or old headboards, wrapped with foam or polyester batting, then covered with fabric. For more ideas and construction details see DECORATING WITH FABRIC/An Idea Book by Judy Lindahl.

Photo James Seeman Studios, Wallcovering: A Div. of MASONITE Corp.

UPHOLSTERED HEADBOARD and padded lambrequin are easy-to-make acessories that add unity and efficiency to this striking room.

EASY SLIPCOVERS

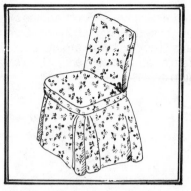

Cooling or warming a room can be achieved in part through the addition of simple slipcovers, throws, runners, quilts, coverlets, etc. Whether the effect is cool or warm will depend on the colors and fabrics you choose. A textured, napped, warm-colored sofa becomes cooler when covered by a glazed chintz or cotton throw cover in cooler colors. Conversely, a summery rattan sofa with cool chintz cushions becomes warmer when covers are replaced with warm colors and napped or quilted texture, or the entire sofa gets a loose slipcover of quilted fabric.

It just takes a little thinking, and perhaps researching through magazines to get some ideas. You'll be seeing more and more of this type of decorating— so keep watching and collect the ideas you like. Clip pictures of pieces of furniture or rooms you enjoy that inspire you and make your own ideas flow.

The softer looks in decor have never made it easier to make seasonal changes in furnishings. Of course, if you prefer or your furniture demands, you can have traditional fitted slipcovers. You'll find directions in many sewing books including: READER'S DIGEST COMPLETE GUIDE TO SEWING ($16.95), SUNSET'S SLIPCOVERS AND BEDSPREADS ($3.95) and SINGER'S HOW TO SEW SLIP COVERS ($1.00).

In addition to the usual yardage outlets try discount outlets for manufacturers of clothing or home furnishings for slipcover yardage.

DRAPE, TUCK, AND TIE
Suitable for softer fabrics that gather and drape.

ONE PIECE DRAPE
Tape measure the chair or sofa, following contours. Measure front to back and side to side from the floor.

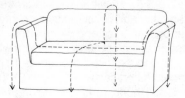

Seam together enough lengths of fabrics to make a drop-cloth 26" *(66 cm)* longer and wider than the measurement. Center the fabric on the chair or sofa. Tuck in deeply around seat. Snugly gather excess at corners. Mark hem around bottom edge. Trim excess and round corners. Fuse or stitch hem in place. Then—

1. Secure with ¾" *(2 cm)* cord. Tie in bows at corners

   OR—

2. Band with a 1½" *(3,8 cm)* strip of matching fabric

   OR—

3. Make buttonholes or attach grommets on each side of the gathers. Thread a cord or fabric strip through and tie in a bow as in next method.

DRAPED FRAME/SEPARATE CUSHIONS

The frame is draped as in previous method. Separate covers are placed over the cushions.

1. Remove cushions and measure, following contours of chair or sofa. Measure front to back and side to side from the floor.

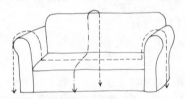

2. Make a drop cloth 10" *(25,5 cm)* wider and longer than the recorded measurements. Drape the fabric over the sofa or chair. Center the fabric and tuck in tightly across the back and along arms.
3. Gather up excess fabric at the corners. Hold folds while you determine tie placement behind the folds. Insert grommets (or make buttonholes) at the marked locations. Insert ties while you mark the hem location.
4. Remove ties, trim excess fabric from hem leaving 1" *(2,5 cm)*. Fuse or stitch hem in place.

5. Make cushion covers from matching fabric. Choose whatever method you prefer from standard pillow covers to drawstring style.
6. Reposition drop, replace cushions, insert ties through grommets.

This same technique can be used on dining or side chairs, ottomans, etc.

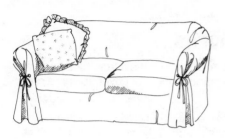

If fabric must be pieced to achieve needed size, consider these locations.

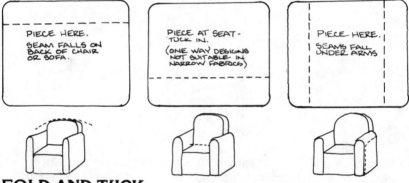

PIECE HERE.
SEAM FALLS ON BACK OF CHAIR OR SOFA.

PIECE AT SEAT - TUCK IN.
(ONE WAY DESIGNS NOT SUITABLE IN NARROW FABRICS)

PIECE HERE.
SEAMS FALL UNDER ARMS

FOLD AND TUCK

These easy covers lend themselves to furniture with basically straight lines and to fabrics with more body such as upholstery fabrics, quilted yardage, mattress pads, movers' pads, or quilts and comforters.

1. Measure as for the draped throws described earlier, but smooth excess fabric into 'hospital miters.' Keep working fabric, smoothing as you go until it lies smooth.

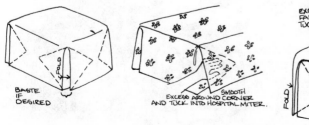

BASTE IF DESIRED

SMOOTH EXCESS AROUND CORNER AND TUCK INTO HOSPITAL MITER.

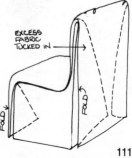

EXCESS FABRIC TUCKED IN

2. Trim at bottom and bind or turn a hem as preferred. Hold folds in place with bands or cords, pins, or hand whip open edges in place.

NOTE: If you plan to wash the covers, it is advisable to pre-shrink the fabrics.

HINT: Mattress pads and other quilted goods can be made into traditional slip covers.

EASY PIN-FIT-STITCH COVERS

Side chairs, dining chairs, folding chairs, etc. can benefit from these simple covers. Cover up winter fabrics with a summer look, or cover up spare cold lines with a cozy padded cover.

1. Rough cut fabric several inches *(cm)* larger than chair back with one piece long enough to extend over chair seat. With wrong sides out, pin fit the pieces to the chair back. Mark seat/seam line on both front and back pieces. Stitch around three sides, starting and stopping the seat/seam line. Trim corners, press and turn right side out.

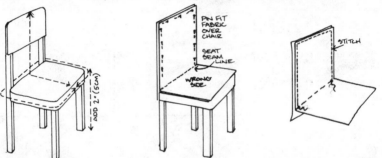

2. Measure around chair at seat line. Double this measurement. Cut or seam fabric to this length and the height of the chair (floor to seat) plus 2" *(5 cm)*.

3. For Ruffled Skirt—
Fuse or stitch a 1½" *(3,8 cm)* hem on bottom edge. Gather the top edge of the fabric and fit it to the back and seat of the cover. Stitch a ½" *(1,3 cm)* seam. Press, turn right side out. Make a pillow for the chair seat if desired.

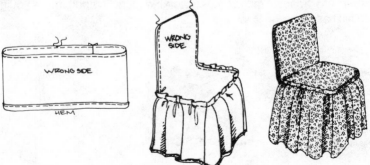

For Pleated Skirt—
Fit skirt to chair back piece with smooth sides and a box pleat at each corner. Pin with right sides together, then stitch a ½″ *(1,3 cm)* seam. Trim corners, turn and press. Add pillow for seat if desired.

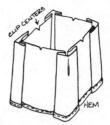

IDEA: Pin fit a quilted fabric cover for just the back of a chair. Bind the bottom edge. Then make a separate pillow cushion for the seat.

SLIPOVERS

Slipovers are flat fabric runners that are laid loosely over furniture. They are simple to make, can disguise damaged surfaces, add color and design, or create a feeling of warmth or coolness. If the fabric has lots of body, one layer, hemmed or bound with trim is sufficient. If the slipover will be seen from both sides, it needs to be lined with matching or contrasting fabric.

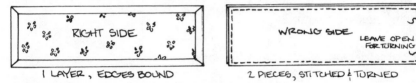

Slipovers are used singly or crossed. Pillows may be covered by the slipovers, or may be covered separately. Here is a collection of slipover ideas:

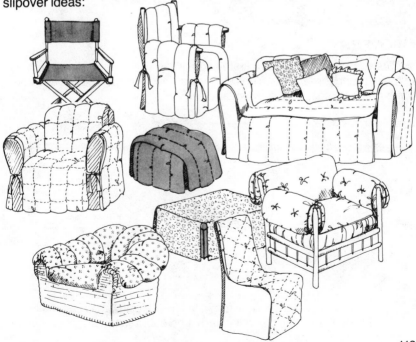

The appearance and wear of the slipover is enhanced when padding is added. A thin layer of Pellon fleece, Thermo Lam® Plus or needlepunch may be added for a little body. Several layers of quilt batting may be used for sofa and chair covers. It is this latter look that is most popular with designers, who also use quilts, comforters, mattress or movers' pads to create the mood.

To make a quilted slipover, follow directions for easy comforter, then either tie or quilt the runner when it is finished. Channel quilting is especially popular now.

To determine length: Measure from floor up and over and down to the floor. Slipovers will fall free, unless you decide to band them or add ties to hold them more securely.

SIMPLE PILLOW COVERS

KNIFE EDGE — easiest of the fitted pillows. Seam two pieces of fabric on three sides. Insert a zipper in the fourth (or whip the opening closed by hand).

Special corner treatments soften their look:

TIE CORNERS

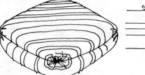

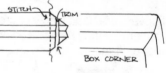

STITCH / TRIM

BOX CORNER

SLIPOVERS

Measure and cut fabric as for a knife edge pillow. Put wrong sides together and sew around three sides. Turn and press. Bind the open edges and add more binding for ties. Slip pillow in, and tie.

WRONG SIDE

ENERGY TIP If you use a reversible fabric or line the pillow, you can make it reversible and use it for warm and cool seasons.

DRAWSTRING COVERS

Chair and sofa cushions can be quickly covered this way. Simply measure the sides and depth of the cushion for both the length and the width. Add 8″ *(20,5 cm)* to each measurement and cut fabric pieces.

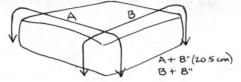

A + 8″ *(20.5 cm)*
B + 8″

Round corners then stitch a ½″ *(1,3 cm)* casing, leaving an opening for inserting a drawstring, or ⅜″ *(1 cm)* elastic.

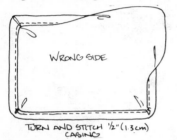

WRONG SIDE

TURN AND STITCH ½″ (1.3 cm) CASING

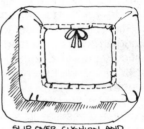

SLIP OVER CUSHION AND PULL UP ON DRAW STRING

WRAP COVERS

This is a modified slipover.

1. Measure as for the drawstring method above, but add 16″ *(40,5 cm)* to each measurement.

2. Cut fabric piece to these dimensions, then remove corner pieces as indicated below. Bind the cut edges of the corner or machine stitch a narrow hem the depth of the cushion.

3. Wrap each flap under the cushion. If desired, whip stitch corners to hold them more securely.

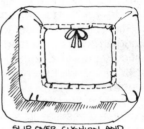

8″ (20.5 cm)
CUSHION DEPTH
CUSHION TOP

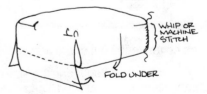

WHIP OR MACHINE STITCH

FOLD UNDER

ENERGY TIP

Make a small quilted mat and attach it over the mail slot with friction fit or magnetic seal. Make a quilted magnetic mat or "friction fit shutter" to cover fireplace opening and seal it when not in use.

LAMPSHADE COVER

This simple technique can also be used to make covers for wastebaskets, planters, etc.

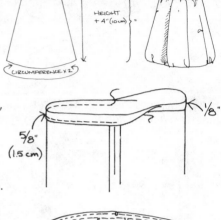

1. Cut a strip of fabric equal to:
   Height of shade + 4" *(10 cm)*.
   Circumference of shade × 2.
   Note: the strip may be seamed
   if necessary. Seams can be
   hidden in gathers.

2. Seam the short ends together,
   then fold the raw edges under ⅛"
   (3mm). Turn the folded edge
   down ⅝" *(1,5 cm)* to form casing. Stitch close to folded edge,
   leaving an opening to insert
   elastic. Repeat with bottom edge.

3. Cut ⅜" *(1 cm)* elastic and run it
   through casings, drawing it up so
   the cover fits the shade snugly.
   Remove excess elastic, sew
   ends together, and close the
   openings by sewing.

AIR CONDITIONER COVER

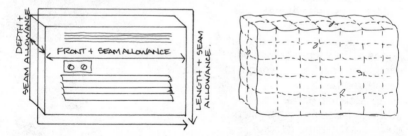

The cover keeps out drafts and 'hides' the unit during off season.

Cut a piece of quilted fabric the size of the front of the unit, plus ½" *(1,3 cm)* seam allowance all around. Cut strips the length and depth of each side plus ½" *(1,3 cm)* along one long edge. Seam to front section. Hem or bind the raw edge. Slip over air conditioner.

LIGHTING

The psychology of warm vs. cool lighting was discussed in chapter one. It is also important to understand the economics of lighting as they relate to size of bulb, type of lighting, size and color of room, type of activity, placement of lighting, etc. Energy savings can be achieved through the wise and careful control of lighting in your home.

ENERGY TIP

The cost of electricity for lighting can amount to 10-20% of your electric bill, so it pays to turn off lights when they're not in use. Keep bulbs and fixtures clean. Accumulation of dust can lower lighting levels by as much as 50%.

Conservation of electrical energy in lighting can be achieved not only by 'watt watching' but also by 'thinking fluorescent.' Fluorescent tubes last 10 to 20 times longer than incandescent bulbs, and they furnish 3 to 5 times more illumination than incandescent bulbs of the same wattage.

Type of Lamp	Lumens (measure of light output)	Life (approx. hrs)
40w incandescent	455-460	1,500
40w fluorescent	1490	18,000

Consequently, a 40w fluorescent lamp can actually be used to give more lumens of light than a 100w incandescent lamp. There are also fluorescent lamps designed to reduce electric energy costs. For example: G.E. 'Watt-Miser,' Sylvania 'Super-Saver,' and Westinghouse "Econ-o-watt."

Circular fluorescent tubes and ballasts that can be screwed into ordinary incandescent sockets are also available. The bare bulb is exposed unless your lamp or fixture has a shade to conceal it; some have an attached 'shade' to make them more appealing. There are also several companies making fixtures specifically for fluorescent lamps, and one company, Home-Vue of Conyers, Georgia, specializes in fluorescent fixtures.

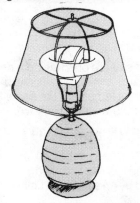

Fluorescent lights diffuse light more uniformly over broader areas and give more comfortable seeing, reduced glare and shadows. This diffusing quality makes them an especially good choice for kitchens, workshop and study areas where a high level of illumination is desirable.

NOTE: Remember also that fluorescent lights 'burn cooler' and give off less actual heat into a room than incandescent bulbs.

RETROFITTING CEILING FIXTURES

Replacing a standard incandescent ceiling fixture with a fluorescent fixture is a simple job. A special feature of retrofit fixtures is the adapter plate which simplifies the installation.

Step I. Turn off current. Remove existing incandescent ceiling fixtures.

Step II. Pull wires through center hole of adapter plate. Fasten plate to ceiling

Step III. Attach fixture plate with nut. Line fixture base up. Use 2 screws (one at each end) to fasten base to ceiling.

Step IV. Insert tubes into fixture base. Snap on wraparound lens. Conversion is complete.

NOTE: If you are purchasing a new fluorescent fixture look for one that incorporates an energy efficient ballast as well as the energy efficient lamp. The efficient lamps are the same length of tube but use less energy (example: 35w instead of 40w).

DIMMERS and SWITCHES

Look for 3-way switches on lamps. These allow you to adjust the level of lighting as it is needed, and you save energy in the process. These can be identified by an aluminum colored tab at the base of the threaded area in the socket.

The use of dimmers not only creates more mood and flexibility in your lighting plan, it is a valid energy saver. Action of the dimmer reduces the light level when higher amounts are not needed by damping down the flow of power to the fixture, thus saving electricity. Bulbs will last longer, too.

Wall dimmers fit the same electrical wall boxes as replacements for standard switches and are available in several types including knobs, dials, pull levers and pressure sensitive plates. Depending on the specific dimmer they range up to 600 watts or more. Table-top dimmers can be added to any lamp and are especially useful on single wattage lamps. Other types include the on-cord dimmer, which can be added easily by the do-it-yourselfer, and the socket dimmer.

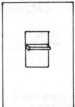

BULB DIAL   CORD DIAL   CORD SLIDE   WALL SLIDE   WALL DIAL

Since the development of solid state controls, dimmers for fluorescent lamps have been simplified and made more readily available. A system consists of a control, a transformer, and a dimmer ballast. The components should be matched, which is accomplished by using parts from the same manufacturer.

ENERGY TIP

Photo electric light controls are more efficient since they turn light on only in the absence of light, rather than at a specific time of day. When selecting or replacing light fixtures, try to choose one that has one large bulb rather than several smaller ones whenever possible. A single 75w bulb uses the same energy as three 25w bulbs and gives 68% more light.

ACTIVITY LIGHTING

Plan activity lighting into your rooms. For example, it is more efficient to provide a good lamp for reading, sewing, bookwork, etc., than to bring the illumination level in the entire room to the level needed for that activity. An excellent source book for detailed information on specific measurements, distances, and bulb size and type is the pamphlet by General Electric, THE LIGHT BOOK (see Suggested Reading), which may be available from your electric utility company.

Place floor lamps or table lamps in a corner instead of along a wall. They'll reflect light from two walls, giving you more usable light for your money.

Accent lighting or spot lighting can be made more efficient by using some of the new portable fixtures such as the 'Miser Spot' by G.E. It uses a 50w reflector bulb to obtain the same light as a standard 100w bulb and it has triple the bulb life. These 50w energy-saving reflector bulbs may also be used in pole lamps and other spot lamps as well. You may wish to try the

25w reflector flood bulbs in high-intensity portable lamps. They provide about the same light but use less energy than the 40w bulb normally found in these lamps.

Wherever possible, use lower wattages, i.e. hallways, storage areas. In hard to reach areas where bulbs need to be changed as seldom as possible, use extended life bulbs. They last longer, but give less light.

Use low-wattage night lights. Now available in 4 watt size as well as 7w, the clear finish 4w bulb gives almost as much light and uses about half the energy.

LIGHTING AND COLOR

Any decorating becomes a part of interior lighting design—because every surface reflects some light. Thus light can be absorbed or even wasted by dark surfaces, or it can be reflected from light surfaces and become useful illumination.

Because light colors reflect more light they require less artificial lighting, hence they can help reap energy savings in less electricity used. This is true of the furnishings in a room, as well. If you love darker dramatic colors rather than lighter pastels, consider using mirrors and reflective surfaces (chrome, brass, mylar) in your decorating. By increasing reflected light you can help compensate for light absorbed by darker colors.

Look at the chart below and see how the level of reflected light varies as the color deepens.

PER CENT OF LIGHT REFLECTED BY COLORS

White	89	Buff	63
Ivory	87	Pale Green	59
Canary Yellow	77	Light Green	56
Cream	77	Shell Pink	55
Orchid	67	Olive Tan	43
Pale Blue	66	Forest Green	22
Sky Blue	65	Coconut Brown	16
Lt. Gray	65	Black	2

NOTE: Keep in mind that reflected light will always be tinted with the color of the reflecting surface. It is this principle that is often responsible for making the color of painted walls appear more intense than the color of a paint chip.

Light makes color 'live.' Low levels of illumination make colors seem greyer, duller and subdued. This contributes to coolness. As illumination increases, colors become more vibrant and alive, adding a warmth factor.

ENERGY TIP Use transluscent lamp shades and avoid opaque or dark shades which block light and waste energy.

VAPOR BARRIERS & INSULATION

The seriousness of the problem of excessive moisture build-up and condensation in walls or insulation is generally dependent upon where you live. Usually, the drier and warmer the climate, the less likely the problem. The illustration below shows the map published by the Federal Dept. of Energy in Nov. 1970. Moisture problems are most likely in zone 1 and least likely in zone 3. The shaded area has no condensation problem during heating seasons, but there may be a problem during the cooling season.

Vapor Barrier Requirements

ZONE I

ZONE I

ZONE II

ZONE III

NOTE: One thing that can CREATE a moisture problem is the addition or creation of a vapor barrier on the outside of the home. Such a problem could be created by metal or vinyl siding over foil paper, or many coats of paint that eliminate the ability of the exterior to 'breathe.' If you suspect problems with excessive moisture passing through walls contributing to peeling paint, staining of interior surfaces, or condensation build-up in insulation contributing to some loss of effectiveness of insulation and dry rot damage, it is advisable to get more in-depth information and formulate your plan of attack. (Suggested reading: SOLUTIONS TO A VAPOROUS PROBLEM, New Shelter Magazine, p. 71, May/June '80.) Seek information about studies done in the area where you live. Contact utility companies, state agencies or universities near you.

In general, the treatment is three-fold: Adequate ventilation, a vapor barrier, and reduction of moisture inside the home. A vapor barrier must be applied on the inside surface of the insulated area to prevent moisture from entering the wall or attic. Since it is neither practical nor economical to gut the room to apply a vapor-barrier, consider interior vapor barrier protection.

VAPOR BARRIER PAINT

When you plan to repaint or recover walls, consider first applying a coat of vapor barrier paint with a low perm rating (see table below) to the inside surface of outside walls or ceilings that adjoin unheated areas. Insul-Aid™ latex by Glidden is one example of a vapor barrier paint that reduces moisture passing through walls or ceilings. According to the manufacturer, tests show InsulAid™ holds in up to nine times more moisture than high quality latex alone, thus giving 20% less heat loss through Insul-Aid™ coated walls compared to uncoated walls. It is also a simple way to retro-fit a vapor barrier to ceilings and helps reduce the amount of ventilation needed in attic areas.

VAPOR BARRIER PERM RATINGS
A perm is a unit designating the amount of moisture which will pass through a substance. A perm of 1 is considered adequate as a vapor barrier: less than 1 is better.

aluminum foil	0.0
polyethylene (4-6 mil)	0.08
1 coat vapor barrier latex paint	0.6
vinyl wall covering	1.0
2 coats oil paint on plaster	2.0
3 coats latex on wood	10.0
Ordinary wallpaper	20.0

WALLCOVERING

Vinyl or aluminum foil wallcoverings can create adequate vapor barriers and are particularly good choices for high moisture areas like kitchens, bath or laundry. If you are planning to cover walls with fabric, consider applying a vapor barrier first. This might take the form of paint, polyethylene or even aluminum foil. Like foil wallcoverings it will reflect a certain amount of heat back into the room.

NOTE: If you paint the ceilings in high moisture areas or those in rooms adjoining unheated space, use a vapor barrier paint first.

 ENERGY TIP To reduce the amount of moisture in the home, keep lids on pots when cooking. Don't dry laundry inside, and do not attempt to dry large quantities of firewood inside. A cord of green wood can contain as much as 2,000 lbs. of water.

INSIDE INSULATION

This technique is gaining ground for some situations, but is generally more than a 'decorating project.' It involves applying rigid type insulation with inside facing vapor barrier over existing walls, then adding wallboard or paneling. It moves the walls forward and requires outlets to be moved outward, hence is not for everyone . . . but it is a retrofit method worth mentioning. Further research about methods and materials is recommended before such a project is attempted.

There are several possibilities for adding ceiling insulation from the inside for problem ceilings with beam construction or where no attic exists, etc. Rigid foam insulating panels may be applied between beams and sheathed over, or there are flexible fire resistant panels of fiberglas with washable, textured vinyl surfaces that can fill such spaces. The fiberglas type (Owens-Corning) is also available in sections to fit in a metal grid system.

James Seeman Studios, Wallcovering; A Div. of MASONITE Corp.

FOIL AND MYLAR as well as vinyl wallcoverings can act as interior vapor barriers.

MOVE THE AIR
—Consider Fans

One of the simplest ways to increase your comfort is through the use of fans and well-planned ventilation that can move the air about your house. Usually, we don't think of fans as decorative objects. An exception is the paddle fan—once thought of only in the tropics or the movie "Casablanca." These slow-turning paddle-blade fans are now touted both by decorators and energy-conservers for their year-round benefits.

In winter the fans work effectively to push warm air that is otherwise trapped near the ceiling, back down into the room distributng heat more evenly. In summer they work basically the same way. But the air-motion created by the fan works like a wind-chill factor causing evaporative cooling against the skin.

Some paddle fan models now come with reversing motors or blades that can be angled upward or downward to change the air direction for summer and winter . . . worth looking for.

Other types of fans can obviously be used as well, and newer decorative types may be introduced. Meanwhile, we can make fans a part of the decorating plan—or simply a practical addition when needed. Even a portable fan can be used to force warm air back to the floor by placing the fan, on its lowest setting, at a slight upward tilt diagonally to the wall.

THE WHOLE-HOUSE FAN: Worth Considering

While the installation of a whole-house fan requires some construction and is not decorative—it is another old concept, re-born that deserves attention from the energy-minded. Installed cost is about $400-600 (less if you do the work yourself). These fans help cool the house by pulling outside air in, creating an artificial breeze to cool house and occupants to within a few degrees of the outside air temperature. They take advantage of the fact that outside air usually drops 10° to 20° at night.

PRODUCTS

The following information is intended to help identify and clarify some of the products mentioned in this book.

- AWNING CLEAT—Small bracket used to wind off shade cords to hold shade in a raised position. From window or shade shops and marine supply, hardware, or home improvement.
- CARDBOARD CUTTING BOARD—Folding, ruled board used for measuring and squaring fabric for shades. Saves time; aids accuracy. From fabric and notions depts.
- CARPENTER'S SQUARE—Metal L-shaped ruler, used to determine perfect 90° angles. Useful for all shades. Available in hardware, home improvement, some fabric depts.
- CRAFT/FABRIC GLUE—Tacky, fast-drying, remains flexible when dry. These make excellent timesavers for working with fabric. Wilhold, Quik, FabTrim, Tacky, etc.
- FABRICS, FIBERS, REFLECTIVE MATERIALS—See section 'About Fabrics' in Windows Chapter.
- FIBERFILL—Loose polyester fiberfill (like cotton fibers) is used for pillow stuffing, etc. Batted fiberfill has stability and comes in sheets so is useful for comforters, window treatments, pads, mats, etc.
- FLEXIBLE MAGNETIC TAPE—a flexible 'plastic-like' tape available in ½" (1,3 cm) to 1" (2,5 cm) and about ⅛" (3 mm) thick. Comes in rolls or strips. Marvelous for seals around windows and other air-leaks. Usually with peel and stick adhesive. May be painted to match decor.
- FLEXIBLE STEEL TAPE—Very thin, very flexible steel tape, usually with peel and stick backing. May be stainless or coated to avoid rusting. May be attached to the window treatment or to the frame to mate with flexible magnetic tape. Forms an air-tight seal. May be painted.
- FOAMBOARD (FoamCor)—Smooth 'tagboard' with lightweight foam layer in the middle. Strong and light. Easily cut into shapes. Available at display, art supply, or lumber stores in ¼" (6 mm) and ½" (1,3 cm).
- FUSIBLE WEBS—(Stitch Witchery®, Sav-A-Stitch, Poly Web, etc.) Meltable webs of synthetic fibers. Placed between objects, heated with iron, they melt and fuse materials together. From fabric and notions depts.
- INSULATING BOARD (Rigid Foam)—Thermax, High R Sheathing, R-Max) Isocyanurate Foam Board, foil faced, high R-value, strong, light, brown foam insulation for shutters, etc. Available at most building supply stores.
- PLASTIC OR CABONE RINGS—½" (1,3 cm) and ⅝" (1,5 cm) are best for Roman shades. Packaged in notions and knitting supplies. Some stores sell them individually. Also may use small metal or brass rings from fishing supply.
- SKOTCH WOOD JOINERS—Sharp toothed clips used for joining two pieces of wood (shutters, frames, etc.). Easy to use and very strong. From hardware stores.
- SPRING LOADED HINGES—Cabinet hinges used for window treatments and board clamps to form edge seals. Amerock #7929, Liberty #103-SL-2 for example.
- UPSOM BOARD—Cardboard composition board. Can be sawed into shapes. Use for cornices and lambrequins. From lumber supply in several thicknesses. 4' × 8' sheets.
- WATER SOLUBLE TRANSFER PENS—(Wonder Marker, Mark-B-Gone™). You can draw right on fabric, then wipe away marks with a well-moistened cloth. Available in notions. Available in notions.
- WEIGHT ROD—A round ⅜" (1 cm) rod or ⅛" (3 mm) by ¾" (2 cm) flat bar can be used for weight in the bottom of Roman shades. The flat bar can seal to a magnetic strip on window frame. Available in home improvement, hardware, etc.

SUGGESTED READING

For further in-depth study of the subjects mentioned in this book, look for the following in stores or libraries . . .

BOOKS-PAMPHLETS

THERMAL SHADES AND SHUTTERS by Wm. Shurcliff, Brick House Pub. Co., Main St., Andover MA 01810. $12.95 Paperback. Over 100 schemes for reducing heat loss through windows. Full of resources and information including very inexpensive and simple techniques.

MOVABLE INSULATION by Wm. Langdon, Rodale Press, 33 E. Minor St., Emmaus, PA 18049. $9.95 Paperback. A guide to reducing heating and cooling losses through the windows in your home. Well written and illustrated. Full of resources and helpful information.

THE SHADE BOOK and DECORATING WITH FABRIC/An Idea Book by Judy Lindahl. These books deal with the endless uses of fabric in decorating and include tips and techniques for getting fabric on almost ANYTHING. Simple to follow, well illustrated. See ordering information, last page this book.

THE LIGHT BOOK, General Electric, Residential Lighting Specialties, Nela Park, Cleveland, Ohio. Check with your local utility company, they may have this on hand.

WINDOW DESIGN STRATEGIES TO CONSERVE ENERGY, U.S. Dept. of Commerce, Supt. of Documents, U.S. Gov't. Printing Office, Washington, D.C. 20234. $3.75. This pamphlet contains systematic survey of approaches to window energy conservation including windscreens, sunscreens, sunshades, exterior appendages, frame and glazine improvements, and interior accessories (blinds, drapes, roll shades, shutters.) No brand names given.

PERIODICALS—ARTICLES

Many regional and national magazines are producing excellent articles on energy conservation—Better Homes and Gardens, Mechanix Illus., Popular Mechanics, Sunset, etc. In addition here are some that deal specifically with the subject.

NEW SHELTER, 33 E. Minor St., Emmaus, PA 18049. Nine issues a year; $9.00. Dedicated to helping make your home more efficient, more productive, and less dependent on 'outside sources.'

SOLAR AGE, Church Hill, Harrisville, N.H. 03450. Monthly; $20.00 yr. Brief articles on developments in solar energy applications, with emphasis on solar heating and cooling.

ALTERNATIVE SOURCES OF ENERGY, Rt. 2, box 90A, Milaca MN 56353. A quarterly publication; $10 yr. Articles, columns, and features on many aspects of energy alternatives; serves as clearing house for exchange of ideas and technolgoies.

NEW SHELTER, Oct. '80, Vol. 1, #7. This edition is full of window information and excellent how-to instructions for a variety of shutters.

The National Solar Heating and Cooling Information Center, P.O. Box 1607, Rockville, MD 20850, (800) 523-2929, In Pennsylvania (800) 462-4983, maintains lists of resources of topics including Solar Manufacturers of Passive Design Products; Shades or Curtains; Solar Bibliography; Insulation; Energy Conservation Bibliography; Insulation Fact Sheet; etc. Write or call for information.

RESOURCES

If you have been unable to locate materials and hardware for your energy saving treatments locally, some of these resources may be of help:

ASTRO TEMP CO., INC., 481-B Irmen Dr. Dept. ESD, Addison, IL, 60101, (321) 628-8450. Astrolar (needlepunch Tyvek) insulating, reflective fabric for windows, bedding, clothing, etc.

DESIGNER'S RESOURCE NW, Dept. ESD, 215 N.W. 22nd Ave., Portland, OR 97210, (503) 224-6050. Batting for upholstered walls, cornices, window treatments, etc. Flame retardant, ½" thick, 48" wide. Also 1" batting in 48", 60", 72". Samples on request.

FABRI TRAK® 59 Willet Ave., Dept. ESD, Bloomfield, NJ 07003, (212) 532-2393. For information regarding your closest dealer handling the Fabri Trak system.

INSUL-SHIELDS (Ptd), Hammond Enterprises, Inc., 12660 S.E. 122nd Ave., Portland, OR 97266, (503) 658-2893. Inside roller shade storm window kits, lumar and reflective roller shades, plastic edge channel by the foot, etc.

KALWALL SOLAR COMPONENTS, P.O. Box 237 Dept. ESD, Manchester, NH 03105, (603) 668-8186. "Do-It-Yourself Solar Heating Supply Shop and Mail Order Warehouse." Comprehensive catalog—$3.00.

MAG FLEX SALES, P.O. Box 7403, Dept. ESD, Salem, OR 97303. 1-800-547-9161. Adhesive backed flexible magnetic tape and flexible stainless steel tape.

MYLAR FILM—Made by King Sealy, Metallized Products Division, Winchester, MA 01890, (617) 729-8300. Write or call for local distributor. Also from drafting supply stores and Solar Usage Now.

PACIFIC IRON'S FABRIC WORLD, 2230 - 4th Ave. So., Dept. ESD, Seattle, WA 98134. (206) 628-6221. Fabrics, hardware, notions for all types of window treatments and home furnishings including: needlepunch mylar, needlepunch, batting, Thinsulate®, insulating fabric, magnetic tape, shade hardware (rings, pulleys, rollers, cleats, etc.).

SEATTLE TENT AND FABRIC, Mariners Square, Upper Level, Dept ESD, 1900 N. Northlake Way, Seattle, WA 98103, (206) 632-6022. Specializing in fabrics for home, marine, recreational use and energy effective treatments. Includes sun and mildew resistant fabrics, #100 100% cotton duck canvas in widths from 30" to 120", needlepunch mylar, solar screening (for interior and exterior use), Foylon, Roman shade hardware, grommets, magnetic tape, rollers, etc.

SOLAR USAGE NOW, INC., P.O. Box 306, 420 E. Tiffin St., Dept. ESD, Bascom, Ohio 44809, (419) 937-2226. "The World's Largest and Most Comprehensive Buyer's Catalogue of Solar Energy Products." Catalog, "People's Solar Source Book," $5.00 shipped bulk rate, $6.00 shipped UPS (6-7 days delivery).

WARM WINDOW, 8288 Lake City Way N.E., Dept. ESD, Seattle, WA 98155, (206) 527-5094 or 1-800-426-7744. Warm Window™ insulating fabric for window treatments, Roman shade hardware including pulleys and lock pulleys, flexible magnetic tape, flexible steel tape, etc.

ZOMEWORKS CORP., P.O. Box 712, (Dept ESD), Albuquerque, NM 87103, (505) 242-5354. Nightwall® magnetic clips, movable insulation systems, Exolite™ acrylic sheet. Nightwall® Spring Fingers™, etc.

SOURCES FOR DOWN QUILT KITS:

- ALTRA, INC., 5541 Central Ave., Dept. ESD, Boulder, CO 80301, (303) 499-2401
- FROSTLINE KITS CO., Frostline Circle, Dept. ESD, Denver, CO 80241, (303) 451-5600
- SUNDOWN KITS, 14850 N.E. 31st Circle, Dept. ESD, Redmond, WA 98052, (206) 883-3997

OTHER BOOKS BY JUDY LINDAHL

DECORATING WITH FABRIC/An Idea Book.

A wonderful collection of practical, economical suggestions and helpful hints for how to put fabric on practically anything. Includes starched walls, quick drapes, pillows galore, folding screens, stretcher bar art, bath accessories and much more. A timeless resource to use again and again. 128 pages.
Revised © 1980 $4.95

THE SHADE BOOK

How to make your own roller, Roman, balloon, and Austrian shades. Five methods of roller shade construction. Easy-to-follow directions, time-savers, notions and hardware information. Energy tips. Lavishly illustrated with line drawings and photographs. Choose from dozens of ideas for hem and cornice accents. 128 pages.
Revised © 1980 $4.95

If you are unable to locate these books locally, write for ordering information to Judy Lindahl, 3211 NE Siskiyou, Portland, OR 97212, USA or enclose $4.95 per title plus $1.00 postage and handling. Canadian orders in US Funds, please.